D0754325

YOU ARE
WHAT YOU LOVE

YOU ARE
WHAT YOU LOVE

THE SPIRITUAL POWER of HABIT

JAMES K. A. SMITH

Brazos Press
a division of Baker Publishing Group
Grand Rapids, Michigan

© 2016 by James K. A. Smith

Published by Brazos Press
a division of Baker Publishing Group
P.O. Box 6287, Grand Rapids, MI 49516-6287
www.brazospress.com

Printed in the United States of America

Library of Congress Cataloging-in-Publication Data
Names: Smith, James K. A., 1970– author.
Title: You are what you love : the spiritual power of habit / James K. A. Smith.
Description: Grand Rapids, MI : Brazos Press, a division of Baker Publishing Group, [2016] | Includes bibliographical references and index. | Description based on print version record and CIP data provided by publisher; resource not viewed.
Identifiers: LCCN 2015045075 (print) | LCCN 2015040686 (ebook) | ISBN 9781493403660 (ebook) | ISBN 9781587433801 (cloth)
Subjects: LCSH: Liturgics. | Worship. | Christianity and culture.
Classification: LCC BV176.3 (print) | LCC BV176.3 .S48 2016 (ebook) | DDC 264.001—dc23
LC record available at http://lccn.loc.gov/2015045075

Unless otherwise indicated, Scripture quotations are from the Holy Bible, New International Version®. NIV®. Copyright © 1973, 1978, 1984, 2011 by Biblica, Inc.™ Used by permission of Zondervan. All rights reserved worldwide. www.zondervan.com

Scripture quotations labeled NRSV are from the New Revised Standard Version of the Bible, copyright © 1989, by the Division of Christian Education of the National Council of the Churches of Christ in the United States of America. Used by permission. All rights reserved.

Portions of chapter 5 originally appeared in "Growing a Healthy Heart" (*Modern Reformation* 24, no. 3 [May/June 2015]: 38–43) and "Marriage for the Common Good" (*Comment*, July 17, 2014, https://www.cardus.ca/comment/article/4247/marriage-for-the-common -good/) and are used here by permission.

Portions of chapter 7 originally appeared in "The Gift of Constraints" (*Faith & Leadership*, September 10, 2012, https://www.faithandleadership.com/james-ka-smith-gift-constraints); "Jubilee: Creation Is a Manifesto" (*The High Calling*, February 22, 2015, http://www .thehighcalling.org/articles/essay/jubilee-creation-manifesto); "Pursue God: How God Pulls Us to Himself" (*The High Calling*, October 3, 2014, http:// www.thehighcalling.org/articles/essay/pursue-god-how-god-pulls -us-himself); and "Tradition for Innovation" (*Faith & Leadership*, June 13, 2012, https://www.faithandleadership.com/james-ka-smith -tradition-innovation) and are used here by permission.

16 17 18 19 20 21 22   12 11 10 9 8 7 6

green
press
INITIATIVE

For
John Witvliet,
co-conspirator

In memory of
Robert Webber,
one of my most important teachers,
though we never met

Above all else, guard your heart, for everything you do flows from it.

—Proverbs 4:23

My weight is my love. Wherever I am carried, my love is carrying me.

—Augustine, *Confessions*

Lovers are the ones who know most about God; the theologian must listen to them.

—Hans Urs von Balthasar,
Love Alone Is Credible

We in America need ceremonies, is I suppose, sailor, the point of what I have written.

—John Updike, "Packed Dirt, Churchgoing, a Dying Cat, a Traded Car"

Sometimes the smallest things take up the most room in your heart.

—Winnie the Pooh

CONTENTS

PREFACE

You've caught a vision. God has gotten bigger for you. You've captured a sense of the gospel's scope and reach—that the renewing power of Christ reaches "far as the curse is found." You have come to realize that God is not just in the soul-rescue business; he is redeeming *all things* (Col. 1:20).

The Bible has come to life for you in ways you've never experienced before. It's almost like you're seeing Genesis 1 and 2 for the first time, realizing that we're made to be makers, commissioned to be God's image bearers by taking up our God-given labor of culture-making. It's as if someone gave you a new decoder ring for reading the prophets. You can't understand how you ever missed God's passionate concern for justice—calling on the people of God to care for the downtrodden and champion the oppressed. Now as you read you can't help but notice the persistent presence of the widow, the orphan, and the stranger.

Now the question is: What does this have to do with church?

This book articulates a spirituality for culture-makers, showing (I hope) why discipleship needs to be centered in and fueled by our immersion in the body of Christ. Worship is the "imagination station" that incubates our loves and longings so that our cultural endeavors are indexed toward God and his kingdom. If you are passionate about seeking justice, renewing culture, and taking up your vocation to unfurl all of creation's potential, you need to invest in the formation of your imagination. You need to curate your heart. You need to worship well. Because you are what you love.

And you worship what you love.

And you might not love what you think.

Which raises an important question. Let's dare to ask it.

1

YOU ARE WHAT YOU LOVE

To Worship Is Human

What do you *want*?

That's the question. It is the first, last, and most fundamental question of Christian discipleship. In the Gospel of John, it is the first question Jesus poses to those who would follow him. When two would-be disciples who are caught up in John the Baptist's enthusiasm begin to follow, Jesus wheels around on them and pointedly asks, "What do you want?" (John 1:38).

It's the question that is buried under almost every other question Jesus asks each of us. "Will you come and follow me?" is another version of "What do you want?," as is the fundamental question Jesus asks of his errant disciple, Peter: "Do you love me?" (John 21:16 NRSV).

Jesus doesn't encounter Matthew and John—or you and me—and ask, "What do you know?" He doesn't even ask, "What do you believe?" He asks, "What do you want?" This is the most incisive, piercing question Jesus can ask of us precisely because we *are* what we want. Our wants and longings and desires are at the core of our identity, the wellspring from which our actions and behavior flow. Our wants reverberate from our heart, the epicenter of the human person. Thus Scripture counsels, "Above all else, guard your heart, for everything you do flows from it" (Prov. 4:23). Discipleship, we might say, is a way to curate your heart, to be attentive to and intentional about what you love.

So discipleship is more a matter of hungering and thirsting than of knowing and believing. Jesus's command to follow him is a command to align our loves and longings with his—to want what God wants, to desire what God desires, to hunger and thirst after God and crave a world where he is all in all—a vision encapsulated by the shorthand "the kingdom of God."

Jesus is a teacher who doesn't just inform our intellect but forms our very loves. He isn't content to simply deposit new ideas into your mind; he is after nothing less than your wants, your loves, your longings. His "teaching" doesn't just touch the calm, cool, collected space of reflection and contemplation; he is a teacher who invades the heated, passionate regions of the heart. He is the Word who "penetrates even to dividing soul and spirit"; *he* "judges the thoughts and attitudes of the heart" (Heb. 4:12). To follow Jesus is to become a student of the Rabbi who teaches us how to *love*; to be a disciple of Jesus is to enroll in the school of charity. Jesus is not Lecturer-in-Chief; his school of charity is not like a lecture hall where we passively take notes while Jesus spouts facts about himself in a litany of text-heavy PowerPoint slides.

And yet we often approach discipleship as primarily a didactic endeavor—as if becoming a disciple of Jesus is largely an intellectual project, a matter of acquiring knowledge. Why is that?

Because every approach to discipleship and Christian formation assumes an implicit model of what human beings are. While these assumptions usually remain unarticulated, we nonetheless work with some fundamental (though unstated) assumptions about what sorts of creatures we are—and therefore what sorts of learners we are. If being a disciple is being a learner and follower of Jesus, then a lot hinges on what you think "learning" is. And what you think learning is hinges on what you think human beings are. In other words, your understanding of discipleship will reflect a set of working assumptions about the very nature of human beings, even if you've never asked yourself such questions.

This hit home for me in a tangible way several years ago. While paging through an issue of a noted Christian magazine, I was struck by a full-color advertisement for a Bible verse memory program. At the center of the ad was a man's face, and emblazoned across his forehead was a startling claim: "YOU ARE WHAT YOU THINK." That is a very explicit way to state what many of us implicitly assume. In ways that are more "modern" than biblical, we have been taught to assume that human beings are fundamentally *thinking things*. While we might never have read—or even heard of—seventeenth-century French philosopher René Descartes, many of us unwittingly share his definition of the essence of the human person as *res cogitans*, a "thinking thing." Like Descartes, we view our bodies as (at best!) extraneous, temporary vehicles for trucking around our souls or "minds," which are where all the real action takes place. In other words, we imagine human beings as giant bobblehead dolls: with humungous heads and itty-bitty, unimportant bodies. It's the mind that we picture as "mission control" of the human person; it's thinking that defines who we are. "You are what you think" is a motto that reduces human beings to brains-on-a-stick. Ironically, such thinking-thingism assumes that the "heart" of the person is the mind. "I think, therefore I am," Descartes said, and most of our approaches to discipleship end up parroting his idea.

Such an intellectualist model of the human person—one that reduces us to mere intellect—assumes that learning (and hence discipleship) is primarily a matter of depositing ideas and beliefs into mind-containers. Critical education theorist bell hooks, echoing

Paulo Freire, calls this a "banking" model of education: we treat human learners as if they are safe-deposit boxes for knowledge and ideas, mere intellectual receptacles for beliefs. We then think of action as a kind of "withdrawal" from this bank of knowledge, as if our action and behavior were always the outcome of conscious, deliberate, rational reflection that ends with a choice—as if our behavior were basically the conclusion to a little syllogism in our head whereby we *think* our way through the world. In all of this, we ignore the overwhelming power of habit.[1]

So we assume that a disciple is a *learner* who is acquiring more information about God through the Scriptures—that serious discipleship is really discipleship *of the mind*. And of course that's true. Scripture enjoins us to take every thought captive to Christ (2 Cor. 10:5) and to be transformed by the renewing of our minds (Rom. 12:2). A follower of Jesus will be a student of the Word, one "whose delight is in the law of the LORD" (Ps. 1:2). If you're serious about following Jesus, you will drink up every opportunity to learn more about God, God's Word, what he requires of us, and what he desires for his creation. You don't just show up for worship and the sermon: you're there for adult education classes; you join a small-group Bible study; you read your Bible every day; you attend every conference you can; you devour books that help you further understand God and his Word; you drink up knowledge. You want to *learn*.

Ironically, this is true even for versions of Christian faith that are proclaimed "anti-intellectual." Many modes of Christian piety and discipleship that are suspicious of formal theology and higher education are nonetheless "intellectualist" in how they approach discipleship and Christian formation, narrowly focused on filling our intellectual wells with biblical knowledge, convinced that we can *think* our way to holiness—sanctification by information transfer. Indeed, that's precisely the conviction behind the ad for the Bible verse memory program mentioned above: If "you are what you think," then filling your thinking organ with Bible verses should translate into Christlike character, right? If "you are what you think," then changing what you think should change who you are, right?

Right?

The Power of Habit

Do you ever experience a gap between what you *know* and what you *do*? Have you ever found that new knowledge and information don't seem to translate into a new way of life? Ever had the experience of hearing an incredibly illuminating and informative sermon on a Sunday, waking up Monday morning with new resolve and conviction to be different, and already failing by Tuesday night? You are hungry for knowledge; you thirstily drink up biblical ideas; you long to be Christlike; yet all of that knowledge doesn't seem to translate into a way of life. It seems we can't think our way to holiness. Why is that? Is it because you forgot something? Is there some *other* piece of knowledge you still need to acquire? Is it because you're not thinking hard enough?

What if it's because you aren't just a thinking thing? What if the problem here is precisely the implicit model of the human person we've been working with in this whole approach to discipleship? What if Descartes was wrong and we've been hoodwinked into seeing ourselves as thinking things? What if we aren't first and foremost "thinkers"? Then the problem isn't just our individual resolve or our lack of knowledge. The problem is precisely our thinking-thingism.

But what's the alternative? If we question the primacy of thinking and knowledge, aren't we going to slide into an anti-intellectualist embrace of emotion and feelings? And isn't that precisely what's wrong with contemporary culture? We've embraced an "if-it-feels-good-do-it" rationale that encourages us to "follow our passions" and act on whatever whim or instinct or appetite moves us. Isn't that precisely why Christians need to focus on *thinking*—to acquire the *knowledge* necessary to counter the culture of impulse?

Well, how's that working out for you? Aren't we right back to our problem? Has all of your new knowledge and information and thinking liberated you from those habits? As anyone who has ever attended a meeting of Alcoholics Anonymous well knows, "Your best thinking got you here."[2]

To question thinking-thingism is not the same as rejecting thinking. To recognize the limits of knowledge is not to embrace ignorance. We don't need *less* than knowledge; we need more. We need to recognize the power of habit.

That's why we need to reject the reductionistic picture we've unwittingly absorbed in the modern era, one that treats us as if we're only and fundamentally thinking things. Instead we need to embrace a more holistic, biblical model of human persons that *situates* our thinking and knowing in relation to other, more fundamental aspects of the human person. We've become so used to reading the Bible with Cartesian eyes—seeing the world through Descartes's "I think, therefore I am" lens—that we see it confirming our intellectualism and thinking-thingism. But on a closer reading, when we set aside those uniquely modern blinders, we'll find a very different model assumed in the Scriptures.

Consider, for example, Paul's remarkable prayer for the Christians at Philippi in the opening section of his letter to them: "And this is my prayer: that your love may abound more and more in knowledge and depth of insight, so that you may be able to discern what is best and may be pure and blameless for the day of Christ, filled with the fruit of righteousness that comes through Jesus Christ—to the glory and praise of God" (Phil. 1:9–11). Notice the sequence of Paul's prayer here. If you read it too quickly, you might come away with the impression that Paul is primarily concerned about knowledge. Indeed, at a glance, given our habits of mind, you might think Paul is praying that the Christians in Philippi would deepen their knowledge so that they will know what to love. But look again. In fact, Paul's prayer is the inverse: he prays that their *love* might abound more and more because, in some sense, love is the condition for knowledge. It's not that I know in order to love, but rather: I love in order to know. And if we are going to discern "what is best"—what is "excellent," what really matters, what is of ultimate importance—Paul tells us that the place to start is by attending to our *loves*.

There is a very different model of the human person at work here. Instead of the rationalist, intellectualist model that implies, "You are what you think," Paul's prayer hints at a very different conviction: "You are what you *love*."

What if, instead of starting from the assumption that human beings are thinking things, we started from the conviction that human beings are first and foremost *lovers*? What if you are defined not by what you know but by what you *desire*? What if the center and seat of the human person is found not in the heady regions of the intellect but in the gut-level regions of the heart? How would that change our approach to discipleship and Christian formation?

Ancient Wisdom for Contemporary Christians

This ancient, biblical model of the human person is just the prescription for a church that has swallowed the bait of modern thinking-thingism. As Robert Webber liked to say, the future of the church is ancient: Christian wisdom for a postmodern world can be found in a return to ancient voices who never fell prey to modern reductionism. Consider, for example, the work of St. Augustine, a fifth-century philosopher, theologian, and bishop from North Africa who captured this holistic picture of the human person early in the life of the church. In the opening paragraph of his *Confessions*—his spiritual autobiography penned in a mode of prayer—Augustine pinpoints the epicenter of human identity: "You have made us for yourself, and our heart is restless until it

rests in you."[3] Packed into this one line is wisdom that should radically change how we approach worship, discipleship, and Christian
formation. Several themes can be discerned in this compact insight.

Augustine opens with a design claim, a conviction about what
human beings are made for. This is significant for a couple of
reasons. First, it recognizes that human beings are made *by* and
for the Creator who is known in Jesus Christ. In other words, to
be truly and fully human, we need to "find" ourselves in relationship to the One who made us and for whom we are made. The
gospel is the way we learn to be human.[4] As Irenaeus once put
it, "The glory of God is a human being fully alive."[5] Second, the
implicit picture of being human is *dynamic*. To be human is to
be *for* something, directed toward something, oriented toward
something. To be human is to be on the move, pursuing something, *after* something. We are like existential sharks: we have to
move to live. We are not just static containers for ideas; we are
dynamic creatures directed toward some *end*. In philosophy we
have a shorthand term for this: something that is oriented toward
an end or *telos* (a "goal") is described as "teleological." Augustine
rightly recognizes that human beings are teleological creatures.

A second theme worth noting is Augustine's locating of the
center or "organ" of this teleological orientation in the heart, the
seat of our longings and desires. Unfortunately, the language of
the "heart" (*kardia* in Greek) has been co-opted in our culture and
enlisted in the soppy sentimentalism of Hallmark and thus equated
with a kind of emotivism. This is not what the biblical language
of *kardia* suggests, nor is it what Augustine means. Instead, think
of the heart as the fulcrum of your most fundamental longings—
a visceral, subconscious *orientation* to the world. So Augustine
doesn't frame this as merely an intellectual quest. He doesn't say,
"You have made us to *know* you, and our minds are ignorant until
they understand you." The longing that Augustine describes is
less like curiosity and more like hunger—less like an intellectual
puzzle to be solved and more like a craving for sustenance (see

Ps. 42:1–2). So in this picture, the center of gravity of the human person is located not in the intellect but in the heart. Why? Because the heart is the existential chamber of our *love*, and it is our loves that orient us toward some ultimate end or *telos*. It's not just that I "know" some end or "believe" in some *telos*. More than that, I *long* for some end. I *want* something, and want it ultimately. It is my desires that define me. In short, you are what you love.

Indeed, we could say that human beings are fundamentally *erotic* creatures. Unfortunately—and for understandable reasons— the word "erotic" carries a lot of negative connotations in our pornographied culture. Thus Christians tend to be allergic to *eros* (and often set up stark contrasts between *eros* and *agape*, the latter of which we hallow as "Christian" love). But that cedes the

---

In the dynamic relationship between love and knowledge, head and heart, the Scriptures paint a holistic picture of the human person. It's not only our minds that God redeems, but the *whole* person: head, heart, hands. Christ takes captive our minds but also our *kardia*, even what Paul calls our *splagchna*, our "inner parts" that are the seat of our "affections."

Contemporary science is starting to catch up to this ancient biblical wisdom about the human person. Scholars at UCLA and McMaster University have been conducting experiments that are shedding light on our **gut feelings.** Their studies point to the way microbes in our stomachs affect the neural activity of the brain. "Your brain is not just another organ," they report. "It's . . . affected by what goes on in the rest of your body."[a] In fact, *Scientific American* reports that there is "an often-overlooked network of neurons lining our guts that is so extensive some scientists have nicknamed it our 'second brain.'"[b]

No wonder Jesus invites us to follow him by eating and drinking (John 6:53–58). Discipleship doesn't touch just our head or even just our heart: it reaches into our gut, our *splagchna*, our affections.

a. http://www.npr.org/sections/health-shots/2013/11/18/244526773/gut-bacteria -might-guide-the-workings-of-our-minds.
b. http://www.scientificamerican.com/article/gut-second-brain/.

goodness of desire to its disordered hijacking by contemporary culture.[6] In its truest sense, *eros* signals a desire and attraction that is a good feature of our creaturehood. Instead of setting up a false dichotomy between *agape* and *eros*, we could think of *agape* as rightly ordered *eros*: the love of Christ that is shed abroad in our hearts by the Holy Spirit (Rom. 5:5) is a redeemed, rightly ordered desire for God. You are what you *desire*.

This teleological aspect of the human person, coupled with the fundamental centrality of love, generates Augustine's third insight: because we are made to love the One who made and loves us—"we love because he first loved us" (1 John 4:19)—we will find "rest" when our loves are rightly ordered to this ultimate end. But Augustine also notes the alternative: since our hearts are made to find their end in God, we will experience a besetting anxiety and rest*less*ness when we try to love substitutes. To be human is to have a heart. You can't not love. So the question isn't *whether* you will love something as ultimate; the question is *what* you will love as ultimate. And you are what you love.

This brief foray into the Scriptures and the ancient wisdom of St. Augustine reveals a very different model of the human person than we typically assume. This model provides a framework for thinking about the task of discipleship, the nature of sanctification, and the role of worship. Let's unpack this through a metaphor that provides a way to "picture" what we're talking about.

Orienting Desire: The Quest to Be Human

To be human is to be on a quest. To live is to be embarked on a kind of unconscious journey toward a destination of your dreams. As Blaise Pascal put it in his famous wager: "You have to wager. It is not up to you, you are already committed."[7] You can't *not* bet your life on something. You can't *not* be headed somewhere. We live leaning forward, bent on arriving at the place we long for.

The place we unconsciously strive toward is what ancient philosophers of habit called our *telos*—our goal, our end. But the *telos* we live toward is not something that we primarily know or believe or think about; rather, our *telos* is what we *want*, what we long for, what we crave. It is less an ideal that we have ideas about and more a vision of "the good life" that we desire. It is a picture of flourishing that we *imagine* in a visceral, often-unarticulated way—a vague yet attractive sense of where we think true happiness is found. It is the vision of which Cosette sings amidst the squalor of Victor Hugo's *Les Misérables*, her "castle on a cloud." Most of us travel through life with less fanciful visions luring us onward, but such tacit, unconscious visions are no less powerful. To be human, we could say, is to desire the kingdom—*some* kingdom. To call it a "kingdom" is to signal that we're not talking only about some personal, private Eden—some individual nirvana—but that we all live and long for a *social* vision of what we think society should look like too. That's why there's something *ultimate* about this vision: to be oriented toward some sense of the good life is to pursue some vision of how the world *ought* to be.

To be human is to be animated and oriented by some vision of the good life, some picture of what we think counts as "flourishing." And we *want* that. We crave it. We desire it. This is why our most fundamental mode of orientation to the world is love. We are oriented by our longings, directed by our desires. We adopt ways of life that are indexed to such visions of the good life, not usually because we "think through" our options but rather because some picture captures our imagination. Antoine de Saint-Exupéry, the author of *The Little Prince*, succinctly encapsulates the motive power of such allure: "If you want to build a ship," he counsels, "don't drum up people to collect wood and don't assign them tasks and work, but rather teach them to long for the endless immensity of the sea."[8] We aren't really motivated by abstract ideas or pushed by rules and duties. Instead some panoramic tableau of what looks like flourishing has an alluring power that attracts us, drawing us toward it,

To be human is to be animated and oriented by some vision of "the good life."

and we thus live and work toward that goal. We get pulled into a way of life that seems to be the way to arrive in that world. Such a *telos* works on us, not by convincing the intellect, but by allure.

So again, it's a question not of *whether* you long for some version of the kingdom but of *which* version you long for. This is true for any human being; it is a structural feature of human creatureliness. You can't not love. It's why the heart is the seat and fulcrum of the human person, the engine that drives our existence. We are lovers first and foremost. If we think about this in terms of the quest or journey metaphor, we might say that the human heart is part compass and part internal guidance system. The heart is like a multifunctional desire device that is part engine and part homing beacon. Operating under the hood of our consciousness, so to speak—our default autopilot—the longings of the heart both *point* us in the direction of a kingdom and *propel* us toward it. There is a resonance between the *telos* to which we are oriented and the longings and desires that propel us in that direction—like the magnetic power of the pole working on the

The human heart is a compass, orienting us to some vision of "the kingdom," our *telos*.

existential needle of our hearts. You are what you love because you live toward what you *want*.

Augustine gives us another metaphor to understand this dynamic: love is like gravity. Augustine wrote centuries before Newton's insight, so the language he uses is slightly different. He puts it this way:

> A body by its weight tends to move towards its proper place. The weight's movement is not necessarily downwards, but to its appropriate

position: fire tends to move upwards, a stone downwards. They are
acted on by their respective weights; they seek their own place. Oil
poured under water is drawn up to the surface on top of the water.
Water poured on top of oil sinks below the oil. They are acted on by
their respective densities, they seek their own place. Things which
are not in their intended position are restless. Once they are in their
ordered position, they are at rest.[9]

We all know the principle Augustine is talking about. Have you
ever played in a swimming pool and tried to hold a beach ball
under the surface? Its tendency—you might even say its penchant
and desire—is to rise to the surface. It is "restless" when it is held
under the water. It keeps trying to sneak up from under your feet
or hands, bursting toward the surface. It *wants* to be floating.
Conversely, when *I* try to placidly float on the surface of the pool,
my weight wants to take me to the bottom.

Augustine goes on to unpack the analogy: "My weight is my
love," he says. "Wherever I am carried, my love is carrying me."
Our orienting loves are like a kind of gravity—carrying us in the
direction to which they are weighted. If our loves are absorbed with
material things, then our love is a weight that drags us downward
to inferior things. But when our loves are animated by the renewing
fire of the Spirit, then our weight tends upward. In Augustine's
striking picture, "By your gift we are set on fire and carried upwards: we grow red hot and ascend. We climb 'the ascents in our
heart' (Ps. 84:7) and sing 'the song of steps' (Ps. 121:1). Lit by
your fire, your good fire, we grow red-hot and ascend, as we move
upwards 'to the peace of Jerusalem' (Ps. 122:6)."[10] Discipleship
should set us on fire, should change the "weight" of our love.

An Erotic Compass: Love Is a Habit

In this alternative model of the human person, the center of gravity of our identity is located in the heart—in the visceral region of
our longings and desires, the gut-level region of *kardia*. It is our

Love is like autopilot, orienting us without our thinking about it.

desires that orient and direct us toward some ultimate *telos* we take to be the good life, the version of the kingdom we live toward. To be human is to be a lover and to love something ultimate.

But we will only fully appreciate the significance of this for discipleship if we also recognize that such love is a kind of sub-conscious desire that operates *without our thinking about it*. In order to fend off the reductionistic cliché that love is a feeling, we sometimes (rightly) emphasize that love is a choice or that, as Clint Black crooned, love is "something that we do." In a certain sense, that's true. But in another sense, love as we're talking about it here—love as our most fundamental orientation to the world—is less a conscious choice and more like a baseline inclination, a default orientation that generates the choices we make.

This is a very ancient and biblical way of thinking about love. In fact, when we look again at Paul without the blinders of thinking-thingism, we'll note something interesting about how he describes love. Consider how he exhorts the Christians in Colossae: "Therefore, as God's chosen people, holy and dearly loved, clothe yourselves with compassion, kindness, humility, gentleness and patience. Bear with each other and forgive one another if any of you has a grievance against someone. Forgive as the Lord forgave you. And over all these virtues put on love, which binds them all together in perfect unity" (Col. 3:12–14).

Paul uses a clothing metaphor to describe the Christlike life. To "put on" Christ is to clothe ourselves in compassion, kindness, humility, gentleness, and patience (cf. Rom. 13:14). And over all of these things we are to "put on" love. It's like love is the big belt that pulls together the rest of the ensemble. But then notice how Paul describes all of these Christlike character traits: they are *virtues*. While we have a vague sense that virtue is an ethical category, we don't have a classical understanding of the concept anymore, and so we miss some of the force of what Paul is saying here. So let me briefly unpack the basics of virtue so we can then consider the implications of Paul's exhortation with respect to love.

Virtues, quite simply, are good moral habits. (Bad moral habits, as you might guess, are called "vices.") Good moral habits are like internal dispositions to the good—they are character traits that become woven into *who you are* so that you are the *kind* of person who is inclined to be compassionate, forgiving, and so forth. Virtues thus are different from moral laws or rules, which are external stipulations of the good. In fact, as Thomas Aquinas points out, there is an inversely proportionate relationship between virtue and the law:[11] the more virtuous someone is—that is, the more they have an *internal* disposition to the good that bubbles up from their very character—the less they need the external force of the law to compel them to do the good. Conversely, the more "vicious" a person or group of people is, the more they need the "stick" of the law to compel them to do what they ought. Anyone who has raised children is intimately familiar with these dynamics. Early on, we need to constantly tell (and compel) our children to do the right thing. We are training their moral sense. But the goal and hope is that, in the process, they are internalizing a sense of the good and will become the *kind of people* who do this without the "stick" of rules compelling them to do so.

In a sense, then, to become virtuous is to internalize the law (and the good to which the law points) so that you follow it more or less automatically. As Aristotle put it, when you've acquired a moral habit, it becomes second nature. Why do we call things "second" nature? Our "first" nature is the hardwiring that characterizes our biological systems and operates without our thinking about it. At this very moment, you are not *choosing* to breathe. You are not thinking about breathing. (Well, maybe now you are. But 99.9 percent of the time, you breathe and blink and digest your breakfast without thinking about it.) "Nature" simply takes care of a process that hums along under the hood of consciousness. Those habits that become "second" nature operate in the same way: they become so woven into who you are that they are as natural for you as breathing and blinking. You don't have to think about or choose to do these things: they come naturally. When you have acquired the sorts of virtues that are second nature, it means you have become the kind of person who is inclined to the good. You will be kind and compassionate and forgiving because it's inscribed in your very character. You don't have to think about it; it's who you are. (In fact, if I have to *deliberate* about whether to be compassionate, it's a sure sign I lack the virtue!)

A key question then: How do I acquire such virtues? I can't just think my way into virtue.[12] This is another difference between laws or rules, on the one hand, and virtues, on the other. Laws, rules, and commands specify and articulate the good; they *in*form me about what I ought to do. But virtue is different: virtue isn't acquired intellectually but affectively. Education in virtue is not like learning the Ten Commandments or memorizing Colossians 3:12–14. Education in virtue is a kind of *form*ation, a retraining of our dispositions. "Learning" virtue—becoming virtuous— is more like practicing scales on the piano than learning music theory: the goal is, in a sense, for your *fingers* to learn the scales so they can then play "naturally," as it were. Learning here isn't just information acquisition; it's more like inscribing something into the very fiber of your being.

Thus philosophers and theologians from Aristotle to Aquinas have emphasized two aspects of virtue acquisition. First, we learn the virtues through *imitation*. More specifically, we learn to be virtuous by imitating exemplars of justice, compassion, kindness, and love. In our culture that prizes "authenticity" and places a premium on novelty and uniqueness, imitation has received a bad rap, as if being an imitator is synonymous with being a fake (think "imitation leather"). But the New Testament holds imitation in a very different light. Indeed, we are exhorted to be imitators. "Follow my example," Paul says, "as I follow the example of Christ" (1 Cor. 11:1). Similarly, Paul commends imitation to the Christians at Philippi: "join together in following my example, brothers and sisters, and just as you have us as a model, keep your eyes on those who live as we do" (Phil. 3:17).[13] Like a young boy who learns to shave by mimicking what he sees his father doing, so we learn to "put on" the virtues by imitating those who model the Christlike life. This is part of the formative power of our teachers who model the Christian life for us. It's also why the Christian tradition has held up as exemplars of Christlikeness the saints, whose images were often the stained-glass "wallpaper" of Christian worship.

Second, acquiring virtue takes *practice*. Such moral, kingdom-reflecting dispositions are inscribed into your character through rhythms and routines and rituals, enacted over and over again, that implant in you a disposition to an end (*telos*) that becomes a character trait—a sort of learned, second-nature default orientation that you tend toward "without thinking about it." It's important to recognize that such dispositions are not "natural." We're not talking about biological hardwiring or natural instincts. Virtues are learned and acquired, through imitation and practice. It's like we have moral muscles that are trained in the same way our biological muscles are trained when we practice a golf swing or piano scales.

Now why is all of this important for our project of sketching an alternative model of the human person? Because if you are what you love and if love is a virtue, then love is a *habit*. This means that our most fundamental orientation to the world—the longings and desires that orient us toward some version of the good life—is shaped and configured by imitation and practice. This has important implications for how we approach Christian formation and discipleship.

Calibrating the Heart: Love Takes Practice

In short, if you are what you love, and love is a habit, then discipleship is a rehabituation of your loves. This means that discipleship is more a matter of re*form*ation than of acquiring *in*formation. The learning that is fundamental to Christian formation is affective and erotic, a matter of "aiming" our loves, of orienting our desires to God and what God desires for his creation.

If I am what I love and my loves are aimed at a *telos*—oriented toward some version of the good life—then the crucial question I need to ask myself is: How does my love get aimed and directed? We've seen so far that to be human is to be a lover, a creature whose way of inhabiting the world is directed and governed by this erotic orientation to what we long for. We've also seen that, in fact, every human creature is designed to find his or her erotic *telos* in the Creator himself, in the King who has met us in Jesus. However, this structure of human existence is no guarantee that we are pointed in the right direction. While being human means we can't *not* love something ultimate—some version of the kingdom—it doesn't mean we necessarily love the right things, or the true King. God has created us for himself and our hearts are designed to find their end in him, yet many spend their days restlessly craving rival gods, frenetically pursuing rival kingdoms. The subconscious longings of our hearts are aimed and directed elsewhere; our orientation is askew; our erotic compass malfunctions, giving us false bearings. When this happens, the results can be disastrous.

In 1914, not long after the sinking of the *Titanic*, Congress convened a hearing to discern what happened in another nautical tragedy. In January of that year, in thick fog off the Virginia coast, the steamship *Monroe* was rammed by the merchant vessel *Nantucket* and eventually sank. Forty-one sailors lost their lives in the frigid winter waters of the Atlantic. While it was Osmyn Berry, captain of the *Nantucket* who was arraigned on charges, in the course of the trial Captain Edward Johnson was grilled on the stand for over five hours. During cross-examination it was learned, as the *New York Times* reported, that Captain Johnson "navigated the Monroe with a steering compass that deviated as much as two degrees from the standard magnetic compass. He said the instrument was sufficiently true to run the ship, and that it was the custom of masters in the coastwise trade to use such compasses. His steering compass had never been adjusted in the one year he was master of the Monroe." The faulty compass that seemed adequate for navigation eventually proved otherwise. This realization partly explains a heartrending picture recorded by the *Times*: "Later the two Captains met, clasped hands, and sobbed on each other's shoulders." The sobs of these two burly seamen are a moving reminder of the tragic consequences of misorientation.[14]

The reminder for us is this: if the heart is like a compass, an erotic homing device, then we need to (regularly) calibrate our hearts, tuning them to be directed to the Creator, our magnetic north. It is crucial for us to recognize that our ultimate loves, longings, desires, and cravings are *learned*. And because love is a habit, our hearts are calibrated through imitating exemplars and being immersed in practices that, over time, index our hearts to a certain end. We learn to love, then, not primarily by acquiring information about *what* we should love but rather through practices that form the habits of *how* we love. These sorts of practices are "pedagogies" of desire, not because they are like lectures that inform us, but because they are rituals that form and direct our affections.

Now here's the crucial insight for Christian formation and discipleship: not only is this learning-by-practice the way our hearts

---

In the Kingdom of Ice is Hampton Sides's compelling account of the failed nineteenth-century polar expedition of the USS *Jeannette*, captained by Lieutenant George De Long. It is another cautionary tale about **the hazards of misorientation**—not because of a faulty compass but because of a mistaken map. De Long's entire expedition rested on a picture of the (unknown) North Pole laid out in the (ultimately deluded) maps of Dr. August Heinrich Petermann. Petermann's maps suggested a "thermometric gateway" through the ice that opened onto a vast "polar sea" on the top of the world—a fair-weather passage beyond all the ice. De Long's entire expedition was staked on these maps.

But it turned out he was heading to a world that didn't exist. As perilous ice quickly surrounded the ship, Sides recounts, the team had to "shed its organizing ideas, in all their unfounded romance, and to replace them with a reckoning of the way the Arctic truly is."[a]

Our culture often sells us faulty, fantastical maps of "the good life" that paint alluring pictures that draw us toward them. All too often we stake the expedition of our lives on them, setting sail toward them with every sheet hoisted. And we do so *without thinking about it* because these maps work on our imagination, not our intellect. It's not until we're shipwrecked that we realize we trusted faulty maps.

a. Hampton Sides, *In the Kingdom of Ice: The Grand and Terrible Polar Voyage of the USS* Jeannette (New York: Doubleday, 2014), 163.

are correctly calibrated, but it is also the way our loves and longings are *mis*directed and *mis*calibrated—not because our intellect has been hijacked by bad ideas but because our desires have
been captivated by rival visions of flourishing. And that happens
through practices, not propaganda. Our desires are caught more
than they are taught. All kinds of cultural rhythms and routines
are, in fact, rituals that function as pedagogies of desire precisely
because they tacitly and covertly train us to love a certain version
of the kingdom, teach us to long for some rendition of the good
life. These aren't just things we do; they do something *to* us.

This means that Spirit-led formation of our loves is a recalibration of the heart, a reorientation of our loves by unlearning all the
tacit bearings we've absorbed from other cultural practices. We
need to recognize how such rituals can be love-shaping practices
that form and deform our desires—and then be intentional about
countermeasures.

You Are What You Worship

If you are what you love, and your ultimate loves are formed and
aimed by your immersion in practices and cultural rituals, then
such practices fundamentally shape who you are. At stake here is
your very identity, your fundamental allegiances, your core convictions and passions that center both your self-understanding and
your way of life. In other words, this contest of cultural practices
is a competition for your heart—the center of the human person
designed for God, as Augustine reminded us. More precisely, at
stake in the formation of your loves is your religious and spiritual
identity, which is manifested not only in what you think or what you
believe but in what you do—and what those practices do *to* you.

In order to appreciate the spiritual significance of such cultural
practices, let's call these sorts of formative, love-shaping rituals
"liturgies." It's a bit of an old, churchy word, but I want to both
revive and expand it because it crystallizes a final aspect of this

model of the human person: to say "you are what you love" is synonymous with saying "you are what you *worship*." The great Reformer Martin Luther once said, "Whatever your heart clings to and confides in, that is really your god."[15] We become what we worship because what we worship is what we love. As we've seen, it's not a question of *whether* you worship but *what* you worship—which is why John Calvin refers to the human heart as an "idol factory."[16] We can't not worship because we can't not love *something* as ultimate.

Our idolatries, then, are more liturgical than theological. Our most alluring idols are less intellectual inventions and more affective projections—they are the fruit of disordered wants, not just misunderstanding or ignorance. Instead of being on guard for false teachings and analyzing culture in order to sift out the distorting messages, we need to recognize that there are rival liturgies *everywhere*. These pedagogies of desire (which we'll explore further in chapter 2) are, in a sense, cultural liturgies, rival modes of worship.

To be human is to be a liturgical animal, a creature whose loves are shaped by our worship. And worship isn't optional. Even a writer like David Foster Wallace, who had no theological agenda, recognized that to be human is to worship. In a famous commencement address at Kenyon College, he put it this way:

> In the day-to-day trenches of adult life, there is no such thing as atheism. There is no such thing as not worshipping. Everybody worships. The only choice we get is what to worship. And an outstanding reason for choosing some sort of god or spiritual-type thing to worship—be it JC or Allah, be it Yahweh or the Wiccan mother-goddess or the Four Noble Truths or some infrangible set of ethical principles—is that pretty much anything else you worship will eat you alive. If you worship money and things—if they are where you tap real meaning in life—then you will never have enough. Never feel you have enough. It's the truth. Worship your own body and beauty and sexual allure and you will always feel ugly, and when time and age start showing, you will die a million deaths before they finally plant you. On one level, we all know this stuff already—it's been codified as myths, proverbs,

clichés, bromides, epigrams, parables: the skeleton of every great story. The trick is keeping the truth up front in daily consciousness. Worship power—you will feel weak and afraid, and you will need ever more power over others to keep the fear at bay. Worship your intellect, being seen as smart—you will end up feeling stupid, a fraud, always on the verge of being found out.

The insidious thing about these forms of worship is not that they're evil or sinful; it is that they are unconscious. They are default settings. They're the kind of worship you just gradually slip into, day after day, getting more and more selective about what you see and how you measure value without ever being fully aware that that's what you're doing.[17]

Wallace sees the inescapability of worshiping but fails to recognize an important feature of human desire: that you can't just *think* your way to right worship. Becoming conscious isn't the only—or even an adequate—solution to the challenge he rightly recognizes. A more holistic response is to intentionally recalibrate the unconscious, to worship *well*, to immerse ourselves in liturgies that are indexed to the kingdom of God precisely so that even our unconscious desires and longings—the affective, under-the-hood ways we intend the world—are indexed to God and what God wants for his world. Through Spirited worship, the grace of God captivates and orients even our unconscious.

We can see hints of this intuition if we go back to Paul's letter to the Colossians. After his exhortation in 3:12–14, Paul turns to a consideration of worship: "Let the peace of Christ rule in your hearts, since as members of one body you were called to peace. And be thankful. Let the message of Christ dwell among you richly as you teach and admonish one another with all wisdom through psalms, hymns, and songs from the Spirit, singing to God with gratitude in your hearts" (Col. 3:15–16).

What Paul describes sounds a lot like, well, the worship of the church, that "body" into which we are called. Now we are in a place to see the connection: we clothe ourselves in Christ's love (vv. 12–14) and "put on" the virtue of love *by* letting the word of Christ dwell in us richly; *by* teaching and admonishing one another; *by* singing psalms, hymns, and songs of the Spirit. The practices of Christian worship train our love—they are practice *for* the coming kingdom, habituating us as citizens of the kingdom of God.

Christian worship, we should recognize, is essentially a *counter*formation to those rival liturgies we are often immersed in, cultural practices that covertly capture our loves and longings, miscalibrating them, orienting us to rival versions of the good life. This is why worship is the heart of discipleship. We can't counter the power of cultural liturgies with didactic information poured into our intellects. We can't recalibrate the heart from the top down, through merely informational measures. The orientation of the heart happens from the bottom up, through the formation of our habits of desire. Learning to love (God) takes practice.

2

YOU MIGHT NOT LOVE
WHAT YOU THINK

Learning to Read "Secular" Liturgies

What do you *want*? That, we've seen, is the question. It is the first and fundamental question of discipleship because you are what you love. But buried in this insight is an uncomfortable realization: you might not love what you think.

Moving Pictures: Two Cinematic Explorations of Desire

This discomforting epiphany is at the heart of Russian filmmaker Andrei Tarkovsky's masterpiece, *Stalker*. The genre hovers between noir thriller and dystopian science fiction. Set in environs that at times evoke Cormac McCarthy's *The Road* but at other moments feel like *The Eternal Sunshine of the Spotless Mind*, the "plot" (such as it is) follows three men on a journey: Professor, Writer, and Stalker, who serves as their guide. As we begin, the destination is shrouded in mystery and intrigue, but eventually we learn that Stalker is leading these men to the Zone, and more specifically to the Room within the Zone. The Zone has the eerie feel of a postapocalyptic oasis, a scene where some prior devastation has left ruins that are now returning to nature, cultivating a terrible beauty, a kind of "bright sadness."[1] (The scenes of this 1980 film are a spooky harbinger of images that would emerge in the aftermath of the 1986 Chernobyl disaster.)

The Room is what has drawn them here, what has led them to follow Stalker's promises. For in the Room, he tells them, they will achieve their heart's desire. In the Room their dreams will come true. In the Room you get exactly what you want.

Which is why, when they are at the threshold of the Room, Professor and Writer begin to get cold feet. Geoff Dyer captures the scene in his remarkable book about the film, *Zona*.

> They are in a big, abandoned, derelict, dark damp room with what look like the remains of an enormous chemistry set floating in the puddle in the middle, as if the Zone resulted from an ill-conceived experiment that went horribly wrong. Off to the right, through a large hole in the wall, is a source of light that they all look towards. For a long while no one speaks. The air is full of the chirpy chirpy cheep cheep of birdsong. It's the opposite of those places where the sedge has withered from the lake and no birds sing. The birds are whistling and chirruping and singing like mad. Stalker tells Writer and Professor—tells *us*—that we are now at the very threshold of the Room. This is the most important moment in your life, he says. Your innermost wish will be made true here.[2]

Here we are. This is the place where you can have what you want. Who wants to go first?

Professor and Writer hesitate because it dawns on them: What if I don't know what I want? "Well," observes Dyer, "that's for the Room to decide. The Room reveals all: what you get is not what you *think* you wish for but what you most *deeply* wish for."[3] A disturbing epiphany is creeping up on Professor and Writer: What if they don't want what they think? What if the desires they are conscious of—the one's they've "chosen," as it were—are not their innermost longings, their deepest wish? What if, in some sense, their deepest longings are humming under their consciousness unawares? What if, in effect, they are not who they *think* they are? Dyer captures the angst here: "Not many people can confront the truth about themselves. If they did they'd run a mile, would take an immediate and profound dislike to the person in whose skin they'd learned to sit quite tolerably all these years."[4]

Many of us can identify. If I ask you, a Christian, to tell me what you *really* want, what you most deeply long for, what you ultimately love—well, of course you *know* the right answer. You *know* what you ought to say. And what you state could be entirely genuine and authentic, a true expression of your intellectual conviction. But would you want to step into the Room? Are you confident that what you *think* you love aligns with your innermost longings? "This," comments Dyer, "is one of the lessons of the Zone: sometimes a man doesn't *want* to do what a man *thinks* he wants to do."[5]

Interestingly, Dyer has an important insight that is relevant to our concerns here. "Your deepest desire," he observes, "is the one manifested by your daily life and habits."[6] This is because our action—our doing—bubbles up from our loves, which, as we've observed, are habits we've acquired through the practices we're immersed in. That means the formation of my loves and desires can be happening "under the hood" of consciousness. I might be learning to love a *telos* that I'm not even aware of and that nonetheless governs my life in unconscious ways.

Christian worship faces this disturbing reality head-on, recognizing the gap between what we *think* we love and what we *really* love, what still propels us toward rival gods and rival visions of the good life. This is why the people of God are called to regularly confess their sins. A historic confession from the Book of Common Prayer names just this tension:

Almighty and most merciful Father,
    we have erred and strayed from thy ways like lost sheep,
    we have followed too much the devices and desires of our own hearts.[7]

The body of Christ is that unique community of practice whose members own up to the fact that we don't always love what we say we do—that the "devices and desires" of our hearts outstrip our best intentions. The practices of Christian worship are a tangible, practiced, re-formative way to address this tension and gap.

This elusiveness of our own loves—the way our desires can elude our conscious awareness—is also illustrated in Alan Ball's Academy Award–winning film, *American Beauty*. Indeed, you could look at the movie as Lester Burnham's *Confessions*: a middle-aged suburban cuckold's quest to "find himself," which spirals into an erotic adventure of looking for love in all the wrong places. In so many ways, the narrative arc of the film embodies the clichéd Hollywood vision of "freedom." At the beginning, the placid, hunched demeanor of Kevin Spacey's Lester listlessly slides through a banal existence in which he is visible only when being nagged by his wife, spurned by his daughter, or berated by his employer. He trudges through life on autopilot, mimicking the herd of "ordinary" suburbanites whose Toyota Camrys are the badge of their selling out on their dreams as nineteen-year-old rebels (despite conforming to the ideal of every other nonconformist). The Man has won; men like Lester have lost themselves—left themselves behind and buried their dreams deep "behind their mortgaged houses."[8] Welcome to the age of inauthenticity.

But then a catalyst arrives in the unlikely figure of Ricky Fitts, a high school senior doing something of a victory lap after spending time away (for reasons that are vague). When his family moves in next door, it quickly becomes clear that Ricky refuses to play the game. He doesn't give a damn about keeping up appearances or living up to expectations and won't submit himself to others' standards. He seems assuredly and prototypically "himself." This, apparently, is what authenticity looks like.

Lester is both humbled and inspired by Ricky's example. One night at a dreary real-estate party Lester is attending with his wife, Carolyn, he is surprised to see Ricky working as a waiter. Ricky invites him out back to do something Lester hasn't done since college: smoke a joint. Hesitant, Lester takes him up on the offer. While they are behind the building, Ricky's boss threatens him: either get back to work or you're fired. "Fine," Ricky says, "I quit." This bold refusal to conform to expectation is an example that Lester will follow. It will appear to be his turning point toward authenticity (though the distinction between appearance and reality proves particularly slippery in this film that exhorts us to "look closer").

Lester, too, will now throw off the chains of familial obligation and moral expectations. To hell with the superego; the id will be all in this rendition of authenticity. And so Lester sets about effectively burning down the parameters of his middle-class existence. He blackmails his boss for a severance package that buys him a year of unfettered "freedom." In a nostalgic move, he sells his Camry and buys a 1970 Firebird, the car of his (boyhood) dreams. And most ominously, he sets about pursuing Angela, his daughter's high school friend. All of Lester's life will now be organized around this longing to bed Angela. Indeed, his imagination is captured by this pursuit: his fantasies are flooded with images of Angela in various states of seductive undress, always bathed and embedded in the lustrous halo of red rose petals.

This turning point in Lester's till-then predictable, ho-hum existence might *look* like his wake-up call to authenticity, his epiphany of self-knowledge. No longer conforming to the expectations of others, Lester has proverbially "found himself" and is now, as our culture exhorts, following his passions. His yearning looks like it will be consummated in a penultimate scene where, alone with a vulnerable Angela, it seems his libidinous desires will be realized. As Neil Young's "Don't Let It Bring You Down" provides an eerie, prescient soundtrack, Lester caresses young Angela and asks, "What do you want?"

Angela, about to be unveiled for the child that she still is, lacks the self-knowledge to answer. "I don't know," she says. "What do *you* want?"[9]

"Are you kidding?" Lester replies. "I want you. I've wanted you since the first moment I saw you."

The scene progresses on its sensuous course until Angela makes her own confession: "This is my first time."

In an instant, the charade of Lester's supposed newfound authenticity crashes like a house of cards. In that moment, the seductive woman who had been the object of his affections is unveiled to be the young girl who could just as easily be his own daughter. Here is the wake-up call in Lester's life; here is the moment of revelation, where the unveiling of Angela's body reveals the disorder of Lester's own loves. Just when he gets what he thinks he wants, he realizes he really wanted something else altogether. And all of a sudden, as we look back on all those fantasies about Angela writhing in rose petals, we remember: it was Carolyn who so tenderly cared for the American Beauties in her garden. And, with Lester, we start to ask ourselves: Is this really what I want?

Under the Radar: Our Unconscious Loves

We have seen that love is a habit. This means that our love is like second nature: it directs and propels us, often under the radar of conscious awareness, like breathing and blinking. It also means that our loves acquire direction and orientation because we are immersed over time in practices and rituals—what we've called "liturgies"—that affectively and viscerally train our desires. So, just as our habits themselves are unconscious—operating under the hood—it is also the case that the process of *habituation* can be unconscious and covert. This is especially true when we don't recognize cultural practices *as* liturgies—when we fail to realize that these aren't just things we do but things that do something *to* us.

Once again, how we think about discipleship depends on how we understand the nature of the human person. We could also say that every approach to discipleship implicitly includes a set of assumptions about how human behavior is generated. If we assume that human beings are thinking things who are always "on," who think through every action and make a conscious decision before ever doing anything, then discipleship will focus on changing how we think. Our primary goal will be informing the intellect so that it can direct our behavior. "I think, therefore I am" translates into a philosophy of action that assumes, "I deliberate, then I do."

The problem is, this is a very stunted view of human persons that generates a simplistic understanding of action and a reductionistic approach to discipleship. It is an approach that unwittingly overestimates the influence of thinking and conscious deliberation and thus tends to overlook and underestimate the power and force of all kinds of unconscious or subconscious processes that orient our being-in-the-world. In short, it underestimates the power of habit. The truth is that, for the most part, we make our way in the world by means of under-the-radar intuition and attunement, a kind of know-how that we carry in our bones. As lovers—as desiring creatures and liturgical animals—our primary orientation to the world is visceral, not cerebral. In this respect, ancient wisdom about spiritual disciplines intersects with contemporary psychological insight into consciousness. The result is a picture that should lead us to appreciate the significant role of the unconscious in action and behavior.

Now, when we talk about the unconscious, try to forget everything you've heard about Freud. We're not talking about Freudian drives or cryptic psychoanalytic myths about your mother. We're talking about what psychologists today would describe as the "adaptive unconscious." Timothy Wilson, a psychologist at the University of Virginia, has described this in his important book *Strangers to Ourselves* (a very Augustinian title!). Over the past twenty years psychology has come to appreciate the overwhelming

Aristotle appreciated that we can't *think* our way to new habits:

> Actions, then, are called just and temperate when they are such as the just or the temperate man would do; but it is not the man who does these that is just and temperate, but the man who also does them as just and temperate men do them. It is well said, then, that **it is by doing just acts that the just man is produced**, and by doing temperate acts the temperate man; without doing these no one would have even a prospect of becoming good.
>
> But most people do not do these, but take refuge in theory and think they are being philosophers and will become good in this way, behaving somewhat like patients who listen attentively to their doctors, but do none of the things they are ordered to do. As the latter will not be made well in body by such a course of treatment, the former will not be made well in soul by such a course of philosophy.[a]

a. Aristotle, *Nicomachean Ethics*, in *The Basic Works of Aristotle*, trans. Richard McKeon (New York: Modern Library, 2001), 2.4.

influence of "nonconscious" or "automatic" operations that shape our behavior—confirming, in many ways, the ancient wisdom of philosophers like Aristotle and Aquinas.[10]

Pointing out the problems with Freud's idiosyncratic concept of the unconscious, Wilson especially emphasizes our failure to appreciate the *scope* of influence the unconscious has on our behavior:

> When [Freud] says . . . that consciousness is the tip of the mental iceberg, he was short of the mark by quite a bit—it may be more the size of a snowball on top of that iceberg. The mind operates most efficiently by relegating a good deal of high-level, sophisticated thinking to the unconscious, just as a modern jumbo jetliner is able to fly on automatic pilot with little or no input from the human, "conscious" pilot. The adaptive unconscious does an excellent job of sizing up the world, warning people of danger, setting goals, and initiating action in a sophisticated and efficient manner.[11]

At one point Wilson wagers that only about 5 percent of what we do in a given day is the outcome of conscious, deliberate choices we make, processed by that snowball on the tip of the iceberg that is human consciousness. The rest of our actions and behaviors are managed below the surface, by all sorts of learned yet now *uncon*scious ways of intending and navigating the world. Psychologists refer to these acquired, unconscious habits as "automaticities," for the same reason Aristotle called them "second nature": because these are ways that we move in the world *without thinking about it.* The language of automaticity isn't meant to reduce us to machines or robots; it's meant to describe how we acquire ways of navigating the world that become built in, so to speak.

Take a simple example: learning to drive. As a parent who has taught four teenagers how to drive (and lived to tell the tale!), I can say that Wilson's insights ring true. When a young person is learning to drive, every facet of this complex activity is managed and executed by the conscious, deliberate "tip" of consciousness. The young driver has to *think* about every aspect: "I need to check my mirrors." "Push the right pedal to go." "The turn signal control is on the left." "Must remember to check my blind spot." "Push the left pedal to stop—with the RIGHT foot!" Add a clutch into the mix and you can imagine how quickly that snowball of conscious deliberation is overwhelmed.

Contrast that now with a seasoned driver. Let's say you've been driving for years, since the day you got your license on your sixteenth birthday. It's a Thursday afternoon. You've just come out of a frustrating meeting at work—a terrible way to end the day. You head straight for the parking lot, replaying scene after maddening scene from the meeting, your blood beginning to boil when you think of how that colleague frustrated you, how another colleague basically stabbed you in the back, and how the manager seemed oblivious to all of these dynamics. You're grinding your teeth now, thinking of all the things you should have said and—lo and behold, you're in your driveway. And you don't remember driving home! How can that be? Because over time, the habits required to drive—to navigate your way through the world—have been repeated over and over again so often that they have seeped into your unconscious and become automaticities. Now you can pretty much drive *without thinking about it*. The complex set of actions required to drive are now managed by the unconscious, below-the-surface aspect of who you are.

The sorts of operations Wilson says are delegated to the unconscious—setting goals, assessing a situation, initiating action—include the "operations" of desire, the "devices of our heart," as the Book of Common Prayer puts it. This is because character and the virtues are also "located" on this unconscious register. The habits we've acquired shape how we perceive the world, which in turn disposes us to act in certain ways. David Brooks captures this dynamic in *The Social Animal*: "The person with good character has taught herself, or been taught by those around her, to see situations in the right way. When she sees something in the right way, she's rigged the game. She's triggered a whole network of unconscious judgments and responses in her mind, biasing her to act in a certain manner."[12] It is in this sense that "character is destiny": your character is the web of dispositions you've acquired (virtues and vices) that work as automaticities, disposing you to act in certain ways.

Your love or desire—aimed at a vision of the good life that shapes how you see the world while also moving and motivating you—is operative on a largely nonconscious level. Your love is a kind of automaticity. That's why we need to be aware of how it is acquired. Now, as psychologists John Bargh and Tanya Chartrand observe, some automaticities are acquired intentionally through "frequent and consistent pairing."[13] In other words, we choose to acquire some automaticities, and the way we inscribe them into our unconscious is by choosing to *practice*. Anyone who can remember learning to play the piano, learning to type, or learning to drive remembers choosing to engage in repeated practice over and over and over precisely so that the rhythms could become habits.

However, Bargh and Chartrand also point out that we can acquire automaticities *un*intentionally; that is, dispositions and habits can be inscribed in our unconscious if we regularly repeat routines and rituals that we fail to recognize *as* formative "practices." So there can be all sorts of automating going on that we do *not* choose and of which we are not aware but that nevertheless happen because we are regularly immersed in environments loaded with such formative rituals. They highlight a powerful example: stereotypes. Stereotypes are just this sort of unconscious, habituated way of perceiving the world and acting accordingly. No one "signs up" to hold prejudiced stereotypes. Instead, they seep into us unawares, acquired unintentionally and yet, over time, becoming habits of perception—automaticities—that govern and guide our behavior.[14]

Now consider the implications of this for what you love. If you think of love-shaping practices as "liturgies," this means you could be worshiping other gods without even knowing it. That's because such cultural liturgies are not just one-off events that you unwittingly do; more significantly, they are formative practices that do something *to* you, unconsciously but effectively tuning your heart to the songs of Babylon rather than the songs of Zion (Ps. 137). Some cultural practices will be effectively training your loves, automating a kind of orientation to the world that seeps into your unconscious ways of being. That's why you might not love what you *think*; you might not love what that snowball of thinking on the tip of the iceberg tells you that you love.

You can learn to love a *telos* unconsciously, in two senses. On the one hand, because your loves are habits, they are mostly operative under the hood, below the surface. So your loves are *un*conscious even though they are *learned*. On the other hand, you can also *learn* unconsciously—that is, the training and aiming and directing of your loves can be happening without your awareness precisely because you don't recognize what's at stake in your cultural immersion. In short, we unconsciously learn to love rival kingdoms because we don't realize we're participating in rival *liturgies*. This partly stems from failing to appreciate the dynamics of the *whole* person, failing to recognize all the below-surface aspects that drive our action and behavior. If you think human beings are brains-on-a-stick, you won't even be looking for these subconscious dynamics. This is the shortcoming of thinking-thingist approaches to Christian discipleship. This reductionistic view of the human person is then mirrored by a failure to see cultural practices *as* liturgies—as habit-forming, love-shaping *rituals* that get hold of our hearts and aim our loves. It's like the opening parable of David Foster Wallace's Kenyon College commencement address: "There are these two young fish swimming along and they happen to meet an older fish swimming the other way, who nods at them and says 'Morning, boys. How's the water?' And the two young fish swim on for a bit, and then eventually one of them looks over at the other and goes 'What the hell is water?'"[15]

We need to become aware of our immersions. "This is water," and you've been swimming in it your whole life. We need to recognize that our imaginations and longings are not impervious to our environments and only informed by our (supposedly "critical") thinking. To the contrary, our loves and imaginations are conscripted by all sorts of liturgies that are loaded with a vision of the good life. To be immersed in those "secular" liturgies is to be habituated to long for what they promise.

Practicing Apocalypse: Recognizing Rival Liturgies

Christian discipleship that is going to be intentional and formative needs to be attentive to all the rival formations we are immersed in. There are two key aspects of this. First, as I've tried to show in chapter 1, we need to become aware of the *whole* person. We need to recognize the power and significance of the preintellectual aspects of who we are. We need to become aware of the importance of the adaptive unconscious that governs our action. Second, we will then see cultural practices *as* liturgies—and hopefully wake up to their (de)formative power. That means looking again at all sorts of supposedly neutral and benign cultural institutions and rituals—things that we do—and seeing their formative, even liturgical power—their capacity to do something *to* us.

Seeing the world and our culture in this way requires a kind of wake-up call, a strategy for jolting us out of our humdrum familiarity and comfort with these institutions in order to see them for what they are. Interestingly, Scripture has a way of doing this: it's called "apocalyptic" literature. Apocalyptic literature—the sort you find in the strange pages of Daniel and the book of Revelation—is a genre of Scripture that tries to get us to see (or see *through*) the empires that constitute our environment, in order to see them for what they *really* are. Unfortunately, we associate apocalyptic literature with "end-times" literature, as if its goal were a matter of prediction. But this is a misunderstanding of the biblical genre. The point of apocalyptic literature is not prediction but *unmasking*—unveiling the realities around us for what they really are. While the Roman Empire pretends to be a gift to civilization and the zenith of human accomplishment, John's apocalyptic perspective from a heavenly angle shows us the reality: Rome is a monster.

So apocalyptic literature is a genre that tries to get us to see the world on a slant, and thus see through the spin. I imagine it a little bit like the vertical louvered blinds in my room. If the blinds are tilted to the left on a 45-degree angle, then from straight on they'll appear to be closed and shutting out the light. But if I move slightly to the left and get parallel to the louvers, I'll find that I can see right through them to the outside world. Apocalyptic literature is like that: the rival empires that would captivate us have something to hide. So you could say they tilt the louvers just slightly to cover what they want to hide. They paint a beautiful picture on the screen, one that captivates and mesmerizes and inspires. If we look at the screen straight on, we're dazzled by what's presented to us. Apocalyptic literature is *revealing* precisely because it gives us a new perspective to see *through* this beguiling (mis)presentation. Apocalyptic literature invites us to lean over and get a new perspective that lets us see *through* the blinders to the monsters behind the screen.

What we need, then, is a kind of contemporary apocalyptic—a language and a genre that sees through the spin and unveils the religious (and idolatrous) character of the contemporary institutions that constitute our own milieu. Too much of our cultural analysis is rooted in thinking-thingism: we scan culture, listening for "messages," bent on rooting out "false" teachings. But if we are first and foremost lovers, and if our action is overwhelmingly governed by our *un*conscious habits, then intellectual threats might not be the most important. Indeed, we could be so fixated on intellectual temptations that we don't realize our hearts are being liturgically co-opted by rival empires all the while. The point of looking at culture through a liturgical lens is to jolt us into a new recognition of *who* we are and *where* we are.

This means we need to read the *practices* that surround us. We have to learn to exegete the rituals we're immersed in. We need to become anthropologists who try, in some way, to see our familiar surroundings with apocalyptic eyes so we can recognize the liturgical power of cultural rituals we take for granted as just "things we do." Pastors need to be ethnographers of the everyday, helping parishioners see their own environment as one that is formative, and all too often *de*formative. The pastor will sometimes be like the old fish in Wallace's parable, regularly asking us, "How's the water?" Eventually we learn: "Oh, this is water."

Let me give you an example—a case study of sorts.

One of my quiet moments of parental success was the day our oldest son, then a young teenager, asked me, "Dad, can you drive me to the temple?" I knew what he meant immediately. We had recently had a discussion in which I tried to impress upon him that the local mall is actually one of the most religious sites in town—but not because it is "preaching" a message or touting a doctrine. No one meets you at the door of the mall and gives you their statement of faith that lists the sixteen things the mall believes. The mall doesn't "believe" anything, and it isn't interested in engaging your intellect. (Its targets are lower.) But don't think that means the mall is a neutral space. And don't think that means the mall isn't religious. The mall is a religious site, not because it is theological but because it is liturgical. Its spiritual significance (and threat) isn't found in its "ideas" or its "messages" but in its rituals. The mall doesn't care what you *think*, but it is very much interested in what you *love*. Victoria's secret is that she's actually after your heart.

So you need to readjust your eyes to see this familiar place. Put on a liturgical lens and look at your local mall again. Read its spaces, its practices, its rituals. What might you see?

Upon approach, the architecture of the building has a recognizable code that makes us feel at home no matter what city we're in.[16] The large glass atriums at the entrances are framed by banners and flags; familiar texts and symbols on the exterior walls help the foreign faithful quickly and easily identify what's inside; and the sprawling layout of the building is anchored by larger pavilions or sanctuaries akin to the vestibules of medieval cathedrals.[17]

We arrive at one of several grandiose entries to the building, channeling us through a colonnade of chromed arches to the

---

A religious studies professor has noted the sacred and religious function of the mall:

> Some of us are interested in religious studies because we are interested in people. People do religious things; they symbolize and ritualize their lives and desire to be in a community. What piqued my interest in shopping malls initially was their concrete expressions of all three of these religious impulses. Quadrilateral architecture, calendrical rituals, replications of natural settings, and attempts to be people, places, and objects of pilgrimage, all illustrate *homo religiosus*. **The shopping mall as a ceremonial center**, the shopping mall as "more than" a marketplace, is one way contemporary people are meeting their needs for renewal and reconnection, essential ingredients of religious and human life.[a]

a. Ira Zepp, *The New Religious Image of Urban America: The Shopping Mall as Ceremonial Center* (Boulder: University Press of Colorado, 1997), 150.

towering glass face with doors lining its base. As we enter the space we are ushered into a narthex of sorts intended for receiving, orienting, and channeling new seekers as well as providing a bit of a decompression space for the regular faithful to "enter in" to the spirit of the space. For the seeker, there is a large map—a kind of worship aid—to help orient the novice to the location of various spiritual offerings and provide direction into the labyrinth that organizes and channels the ritual observance of the pilgrims. (One can readily recognize the regulars, the faithful, who enter the space with a sense of achieved familiarity, who know the rhythms by heart because of habit-forming repetition.)

The design of the interior is inviting to an almost excessive degree, drawing both seekers and the faithful into the enclosed interior spaces, with windows on the ceiling open to the sky but none on the walls open to the surrounding moat of automobiles. The sense conveyed is one of vertical or transcendent openness that at the same time shuts off the clamor and distractions of the horizontal, mundane world. This architectural mode of enclosure and enfolding suggests sanctuary, retreat, and escape. From the narthex entry one is invited to lose oneself in this space that channels the pilgrim into a labyrinth of octagons and circles, inviting a wandering that seems to escape from the driven, goal-oriented ways we inhabit the "outside" world. The pilgrim is also invited to escape from the mundane ticking of clock-time to inhabit a space governed by a different time, even a sort of timelessness. With few windows and a curious baroque manipulation of light, it almost seems as if the sun stands still in this space as we lose consciousness of time's passing and so lose ourselves in the rituals for which we've come. However, while daily clock-time is suspended, the worship space is still governed by a kind of liturgical, festal calendar, variously draped in the colors, symbols, and images of an unending litany of holidays and festivals—to which new ones are regularly added, since the establishment of each new festival translates into greater numbers of pilgrims joining the processions to the sanctuary and engaging in worship.

The layout of this temple has architectural echoes that hearken back to medieval cathedrals—mammoth religious spaces designed to absorb all kinds of religious activities happening at one time. And so one might say that this religious building has a winding labyrinth for contemplation, alongside of which are innumerable chapels devoted to various saints. As we wander the labyrinth in contemplation, preparing to enter one of the chapels, we'll be struck by the rich iconography that lines the walls and interior spaces. Unlike the flattened depictions of saints one might find in stained-glass windows, here one finds an array of three-dimensional icons adorned in garb that—as with all iconography—inspires our desire to be imitators of these exemplars. These statues and icons (mannequins) embody for us concrete images of the good life. These are the ideals of perfection to which we will learn to aspire.[18]

This temple—like countless others now emerging around the world—offers a rich, embodied visual mode of evangelism that *attracts* us. This is a gospel whose power is *beauty*, which speaks to our deepest desires. It compels us to come, not through dire moralisms, but rather with a winsome invitation to share in this envisioned good life.

As we pause to reflect on some of the icons on the outside of one of the chapels, we are thereby invited to consider what's happening *within*—invited to enter into the act of worship more properly, invited to taste and see. We are greeted by a welcoming acolyte who offers to shepherd us through the experience, but also has the wisdom to allow us to explore on our own terms if we so choose. Sometimes we will enter cautiously, curiously, tentatively making our way through this labyrinth within the labyrinth, having a vague sense of need but unsure of how it will be fulfilled, and so open to surprise, to that moment where the spirit leads us to an experience we couldn't have anticipated. Having a sense

A look inside a worship space near you.

of our need, we come looking, not sure what for, but *expectant*, knowing that what we need must be here. And then we hit upon it; combing through the racks, we find the experience and offering that will provide fulfillment. At other times our worship is intentional, directed, and resolute: we have come prepared for just this moment, knowing exactly why we're here, in search of exactly what we need.

In either case, after time spent focusing on and searching in what the faithful call "the racks," with our newfound holy object in hand, we proceed to the altar that is the consummation of worship. While acolytes and other worship assistants have helped us navigate our experience, behind the altar is the priest who presides over the consummating transaction. And this is a religion of transaction, of exchange and communion. When invited to worship here, we are not only invited to give; we are invited to take. We don't leave this transformative experience with just good feeling or pious generalities, but rather with something concrete and tangible—with newly minted relics, as it were, which are themselves the means to the good life embodied in the icons who invited us into this participatory moment in the first place. And so we make our sacrifice, leave our donation, but get in return something with solidity that is wrapped in the colors and symbols of the saints and the season. Released by the priest with a benediction, we make our way out of the chapel in a kind of denouement, not necessarily with the intention of leaving (our awareness of time has been muted), but rather to continue contemplation and be invited into another chapel. Who could resist the tangible realities of the good life so abundantly and invitingly offered?

The point of all this is to try to appreciate how a worldview—or better, what philosopher Charles Taylor calls a "social imaginary"[19]— is "carried" in everyday rituals and practices. How do we learn to be consumerists? Not because someone comes along and offers an argument for why stuff will make me happy. I don't *think* my way into consumerism. Rather, I'm covertly conscripted into a way of life because I have been *formed* by cultural practices that are nothing less than secular liturgies. My loves have been automated by rituals I didn't even realize were liturgies. These tangible, visceral, repeated practices carry a story about human flourishing that we learn in unconscious ways. These practices are loaded with their own teleological orientation toward a particular vision of the good life, a rival version of the kingdom, and by our immersion in them we are—albeit unwittingly—being taught what and how to *love*.

We could repeat such "liturgical" readings of cultural practices for an entire array of everyday rituals. When you put on these liturgical lenses, you'll see the stadium in a whole new way, as a temple of nationalism and militarism. When you look at the university with liturgical eyes, you'll start to realize that the "ideas" and "messages" of the university are often less significant than the rituals of frat parties and campus athletics.[20] When we stop worrying about smartphones just in terms of content (*what* we're looking at) and start to consider the rituals that tether us to them throughout the day, we'll notice that the very form of the practice comes loaded with an egocentric vision that makes *me* the center of the universe.

And so on, and so on. You will begin to appreciate that all sorts of things we do are, when seen in this light, doing something *to* us. It's not just the messages or ideas or information being disseminated by these cultural institutions that have import for discipleship; it is the very form of the practices themselves, their liturgical power to (de)form. Liturgies work affectively and aesthetically—they grab hold of our guts through the power of image, story, and metaphor. That's why the most powerful liturgies are attuned to our embodiment; they speak to our senses; they get under our skin. The way to the heart is through the body, you could say.

How to Read Secular Liturgies: An Exegesis of the Consumer Gospel

"Liturgy," as I'm using the word, is a shorthand term for those rituals that are loaded with an ultimate Story about who we are and what we're for. They carry within them a kind of ultimate orientation. To return to our metaphor above, think of these liturgies as calibration technologies: they bend the needle of our hearts. But when such liturgies are *dis*ordered, aimed at rival kingdoms, they are pointing us away from our magnetic north in Christ. Our loves and longings are steered wrong, not because we've been hoodwinked by bad ideas, but because we've been immersed in de-formative liturgies and not realized it. As a result, we absorb a very different Story about the *telos* of being human and the norms for flourishing. We start to live toward a rival understanding of the good life.

Let's take the example of the mall again as a kind of case study and try to "read" its liturgies more carefully, to read between the lines of the practices and try to discern the social imaginary that is carried in its liturgies. I think we'll notice several features of the mall's version of the kingdom.

1. *I'm broken, therefore I shop.* Given the smiling faces that peer at us from beer commercials and the wealthy people who populate the world of sitcoms, we are sometimes prone to suppose that the culture of consumerism is one of unbridled optimism, looking at the world through rose-colored glasses. But this misses an important element of the mall's rituals—its own construal of the brokenness of the world, which issues not in confession but in consumption. One might say that this is the mall's equivalent of "sin" (though only superficially). The point is this: implicit in those visual icons of success, happiness, pleasure, and fulfillment is a stabbing albeit unarticulated recognition that *that's not me.* We see these images on a billboard or moving in a sitcom, and an implicit recognition seeps into our adaptive unconscious (though, of course, the point is that we never really *articulate* this): "Huh," we think. "Everything seems to work out for these people. They seem to enjoy the good life. Their life is not without its drama and struggles, but they seem to be enjoying family and friends who help them overcome adversity. And they sure have nice accessories to go with all that. Maybe at least part of the reason they're happy

has to do with what surrounds them. That sitcom dad has one of those mammoth chrome BBQs that could grill an entire side of beef in one go; who wouldn't be happier with something like that? That commercial kid has the latest smartphone that keeps him connected at lightning speed; who wouldn't be happier if it were that easy to stay in touch with friends? That billboard mom has it all together. Her kids are smiling and seem remarkably obedient; she's coiffed and slim and seems so carefree—surely that new minivan with the DVD player and fourteen cupholders must have something to do with it." And so on.

Do you see how the images of happiness, fulfillment, and pleasure are actually insinuating something? "This isn't you," they tell us. "And you know it. So do we." What is covertly communicated to us is the disconnect and difference between their lives and our own life, which often doesn't look or feel nearly as chipper and fulfilled as the lives of the people in these images do. The insinuation is that there's something wrong with us, which only exacerbates what we often already feel about ourselves. Of course sometimes this is more direct, like in ads for pimple cream or diet pills—usually not much oblique beating around the bush there, but rather direct, painful charges: "Do you find yourself alone at high school dances because of tumor-sized zits all over your face?" You get the picture. But usually the liturgies of the mall and market inscribe in us a sense that something's wrong with us, that something's broken, by holding up for us the ideals of which we fall short.

On the one hand, those ideals draw on the power of authentic human desires—for friendship, joy, love, and play. On the other hand, they tend to implant and exaggerate less laudable ideals about beauty, power, and privilege. So at the same time that these "perfect" images, these icons of happiness, are subliminally telling me what's wrong with myself, they are also valorizing ideals that run counter to *shalom*—the Bible's shorthand term to describe a flourishing creation, a world that realizes everything God desires for it.[21] As such, the liturgies of the market and mall convey a stealthy message about my own brokenness (and hence a veritable need for redemption), but they do so in a way that plays off the power of shame and embarrassment.

2. *I shop with others.* It is something of a truism that consumerism is an expression of individualism—of both self-interest and self-absorption. But this perhaps misses a certain kind of relationality and sociality that attends the mall's liturgies. After all, it does seem that going to the mall is often a social phenomenon, something one does with others, sometimes even *in order* to be with others. However, what sort of vision of human relationships is implicit in the rituals of the market? While we might participate in the mall's liturgies in pairs or groups, what model of human interaction is implicit in the Story it's selling us? It seems to me that, despite being a site of congregation and even a venue for a certain kind of friendship, in fact its practices inculcate an understanding of human interaction that fosters competition rather than community; it inscribes in us habits of objectification rather than other-regarding love.

Because of the mall's emphasis on ideals of image, and because we are immersed in such ideals almost everywhere, these slowly seep into our fundamental way of perceiving the world. As a result, we not only judge ourselves against that standard, but we fall into the habit of evaluating others by these same standards. For example, if we could somehow analyze ourselves as a friend of a friend approaches "our circle" for the first time, we might catch ourselves looking him up and down or find ourselves taking a quick assessment of how au courant she is in terms of fashion and accessories. I can't tell you how many times I've watched the circle of young women around my daughter and noted the lightning fast up-down assessment, or watched as one of them looks at her shoes and purse while they *think* no one else is looking.[22]

What's just happened in those habits of unstated judgment and evaluation? Two things, it seems to me. First, we've implicitly evaluated others vis-à-vis ourselves and then triangulated this against the ideals we've absorbed from the mall's evangelism. Second, in doing so, we've kept a running score in our head: either we've congratulated ourselves on having won this or that particular comparison or we're demoralized to realize that, once again, we don't measure up. Subtly, then, we've construed our relationships largely in terms of competition—against one another and against the icons of the ideal that have been painted for us. In the process, we have also objectified others: we have turned them into artifacts for observation and evaluation, things to be looked at—and by playing this game, we've also turned ourselves into similar sorts of objects and evaluated ourselves on the basis of our success at being objects worth looking at. While the mall touts itself as a "third place" for friendship, it breeds human interaction that is, at root, a form of competition. We have to unlearn the habits of consumerism in order to learn how to be friends.

3. *I shop (and shop and shop . . .), therefore I am.* If these icons of the ideal subtly impress upon us what's wrong with us and where we fail, then the market's liturgies are really an invitation to rectify the problem. They hold out a sort of redemption *in and through* the goods and services the market provides. Goods and services will save you.

The mall holds out consumption *as* redemption in two senses. In one sense, the shopping itself is construed as a kind of therapy, a healing activity, a way of dealing with the sadness and frustrations of our broken world. The mall offers a sanctuary and a respite that—at least for a time—cover over the doldrums of our workaday existence. So the very activity of shopping is idealized as a means of quasi redemption.

In another sense, the *goal* of shopping is the acquisition of goods and the enjoyment of services that try to address what's wrong with us—our pear-shaped figure; our pimply face; our drab, outdated wardrobe; our rusting old car; and so on. To shop is to seek and to find: we come with a sense of need (given our failure to measure up to its iconic ideals), and the mall promises something to address that. The narratives of the mall's outreach, the veritable stained-glass presentations of the happy life, implant within us a desire to find *that* version of "the kingdom," the good life, which requires acquisition of all the accoutrements in order to secure the ideal and combat our failures.

But, of course, here's the dirty little secret, which we get intimations of but are encouraged to quickly forget: when the shopping excursion is over and all the bags are brought into the house as the spoils of our adventure, we find that we've come back to the same old "real world" we left. The thrill of the shopping experience is over and we now have to do our homework, cut the grass, and wash the dishes.[23] (When can we go again?!) And while the new product has a glitz and fascination about it for a little while, we know (but hate to admit) that the dazzle fades pretty quickly. The new jacket we couldn't wait to wear to school somehow already seems a bit dingy in just a couple of months (or less); the latest and greatest mobile phone that seemed to have "everything" when we got it in the fall is already lacking something by the summer; the video game that we were craving sits unplayed after only a few weeks because we've already beaten every level. In short, what sparkled with the thrill of the new in the mall's slanted light quickly becomes flat and dull. It's not working anymore. And yet: to whom else shall we go? So when can we go again?

This is why the mall's liturgy is not just a practice of acquisition; it is a practice of *consumption*. Its quasi redemption lives off of two ephemeral elements: the thrill of the unsustainable experience or event and the sheen of the novel and new. Both of these are subject to a law of diminishing returns, and neither can last. They both slip away, requiring new experiences and new acquisitions. And the by-product of such persistent acquisition is a side we don't see or talk about much: the necessary *disposal* of the old and boring. So while the liturgy of the market invests products with an almost transcendent sheen and glow, enchanting them with a kind of magic and pseudograce, the strange fact is

We often hear of brand loyalty, even brand "devotion." But do people really *worship* brands? Is consumerism really such a "liturgical" experience? It may not be as far fetched as you think. In a recent study to consider the effect of "super brands" such as Apple and Facebook, researchers made an intriguing discovery. When they analyzed the brain activity of product fanatics, like members of the Apple cult, they found that "the Apple products are triggering the same bits of [their] brain as religious imagery triggers in a person of faith."[a] **This is your brain on Apple**: it looks like it's worshiping.

a. Trevor Mogg, "Apple Causes 'Religious' Reaction in Brains of Fans, Say Neuroscientists," *Digital Trends*, May 18, 2011, http://www.digitaltrends.com/computing/apple-causes-religious-reaction-in-brains-of-fans-say-neuroscientists/.

that the same liturgies encourage us to quickly dispense with these products in a heartbeat. What the mall valorizes as sacred today will be profaned tomorrow as "*so* five minutes ago." Hence the irony that consumerism, which we often denounce as "materialism," is in fact quite happy to reduce things to nothingness. What makes such serial acquisition consumptive is precisely this treatment of things as disposable. While on the one hand this practice invests things with redemptive promise, on the other hand they can never measure up to that promise and so must be discarded for new things that hold out the same (unsustainable) promise.

By our immersion in this liturgy of consumption, we are being trained to both overvalue and undervalue things: we're being trained to invest them with a meaning and significance as objects of love and desire in which we place disproportionate hopes (Augustine would say we are hoping to *enjoy* them when we should only be *using* them) while at the same time treating them (as well as the labor and raw materials that go into them) as easily discarded.

4. *Don't ask, don't tell.* The rituals of the mall and the liturgies of consumption that both sacralize and profane things have another element of ethereality about them: they live off of a kind of invisibility. Just as the mall's structure itself is a haven and

sanctuary, insulated from the noise of traffic and even the movement of the sun, so the liturgies of consumption induce in us a learned ignorance. In particular, they don't want us to ask, "Where does all this stuff come from?" Instead, they encourage us to accept a certain magic, the myth that the garments and equipment that circulate from the mall through our homes and into the landfill simply emerged in shops as if dropped by aliens. The processes of production and transport remain hidden and invisible, like the entrances and exits for the characters at Disney World. This invisibility is not accidental; it is necessary in order for us not to see that this way of life is unsustainable and selfishly lives off the backs of those in the majority world. What the liturgy of the mall trains us to desire as the good life and "the American way" requires such massive consumption of natural resources and cheap (exploitive) labor that it is impossible for this way of life to be universalized. (Though those of us who live in the United States make up only 5 percent of the world's population, we consume somewhere between 23 and 26 percent of the world's energy.)[24] The liturgy of consumption births in us a desire for a way of life that is destructive of creation itself; moreover, it births in us a desire for a way of life that we can't feasibly extend to others, creating a system of privilege and exploitation. In short, the only way for the vision of this kingdom to be a reality is if we keep it to ourselves. The mall's liturgy fosters habits and practices that are unjust, so it does everything it can to prevent us from asking such questions. Don't ask, don't tell; just consume.

Take a Liturgical Audit of Your Life

Now, of course, none of this is announced when you go to the mall. None of these messages are printed on the back of your Gap receipt. Starbucks doesn't adorn its cups with the tagline "I consume, therefore I am." Indeed, to the contrary, for a while Starbucks invited you to sign up for its own liturgical rhythms:

"Take comfort in rituals," the campaign exhorted. The point is that the tenets of a consumer gospel are caught rather than taught; the ideals are carried in the practices, not disseminated through messages. The same is true for other cultural liturgies. The list of such "secular" liturgies is very contextual and will vary not only from country to country but from generation to generation. This is why pastors need to be ethnographers, helping their congregations name and "exegete" their local liturgies.

To recognize this is to appreciate something about the mechanics of temptation: not all sins are decisions. Because we tend to be intellectualists who assume that we are thinking things, we construe temptation and sin accordingly: we think temptation is an intellectual reality, where some idea is presented to us that we then think about and make a conscious choice to pursue (or not). But once you realize that we are not just thinking things but creatures of habit, you'll then realize that temptation isn't just about bad ideas or wrong decisions; it's often a factor of de-formation and wrongly ordered habits. In other words, our sins aren't just discrete, wrong actions and bad decisions; they reflect *vices*.[25] And overcoming them requires more than just knowledge; it requires rehabituation, a re-formation of our loves.

One place to start is simply to become aware of the everyday liturgies in your life. Once you've cultivated the sort of apocalyptic angle on cultural practices that we discussed above and have begun to read your daily rhythms through a liturgical lens, you're then in a place to undertake a kind of liturgical audit of your life. You could think of this as a macro version of the Daily Examen, a spiritual practice inherited from St. Ignatius of Loyola.[26] The Examen is a practice for paying attention to your life: reflect on God's presence; review your day in a spirit of gratitude; become aware of your emotions before God; pray over one feature of your day; and then intentionally look forward to tomorrow.

Imagine a Liturgical Examen to go along with this: Find time to pause for reflection on the rituals and rhythms of your life.

This could even be the focus of an annual retreat. Look at your daily, weekly, monthly, and annual routines. What are the things you do that do something *to* you? What are the secular liturgies in your life? What vision of the good life is carried in those liturgies? What Story is embedded in those cultural practices? What kind of person do they want you to become? To what kingdom are these rituals aimed? What does this cultural institution want you to *love*?

When you see something like the mall through a liturgical lens, you begin to see it very differently. You begin to appreciate what's at stake in this ubiquitous feature of our cultural landscape that perhaps never garnered your attention before. You begin to sense how the mall is a *formative* space, covertly shaping our loves and longings. You begin to realize that what you want has probably been inscribed in the habits you've learned at this temple. You start to sense that this is a place where you've learned (what) to love. And you start getting worried.

Good. That's where we need to begin. We can be led to more intentional Christian discipleship through the back door, so to speak. Waking up to the formative power of secular liturgies might open us up to appreciate the importance of Christian liturgies that we have resisted or perhaps even denounced. A liturgical lens might also give us a new way to see historic Christian worship as a gift. Let's turn to this in chapter 3.

3

THE SPIRIT MEETS YOU WHERE YOU ARE

Historic Worship for a Postmodern Age

Hungry Hearts and Acquired Tastes: Rehabituating Our Hungers

Our hearts, we've said, are like existential compasses and embodied homing beacons: our loves are pulled magnetically to some north toward which our hearts have been calibrated. Our actions and behavior—indeed, a whole way of life—are pulled out of us by this attraction to some vision of the good life. Liturgies, then, are calibration technologies. They train our loves by aiming them toward a certain *telos*. But not all liturgies are created equal: some miscalibrate our hearts, pointing us off course toward pseudo or rival norths. But fixing such disoriented heart-compasses requires recalibration. If our loves can be disordered by secular liturgies, it's also true that our loves need to be reordered (recalibrated) by counterliturgies—embodied, communal practices that are "loaded" with the gospel and indexed to God and his kingdom.

If the orienteering metaphor of the heart-as-compass doesn't quite resonate with you, consider another, suggested by the theologian-troubadour Bruce Springsteen: "Everybody's got a hungry heart." The Scriptures suggest this hunger metaphor as well (Ps. 42:1–2), picturing our deepest longings as a kind of hunger or craving or thirst, a spiritual equivalent to a biological aspect of our being. Think of the beautiful protogospel invitation in Isaiah 55:1:

> Come, all you who are thirsty,
>   come to the waters;
> and you who have no money,
>   come, buy and eat!
> Come, buy wine and milk
>   without money and without cost.

Indeed, in the Sermon on the Mount Jesus extols such hunger as "blessed." "Blessed are those who hunger and thirst for righteousness, for they will be filled" (Matt. 5:6). And Jesus offers himself as the only satisfaction of such hunger: "I am the bread of life. Whoever comes to me will never go hungry, and whoever believes in me will never be thirsty" (John 6:35). If the heart is like a stomach (another reason to affirm "gut" as a contemporary translation of *kardia*!), we could render Augustine's prayer in line with this metaphor: "You have made us for yourself, and our gut will rumble until we feed on you."

There's more going on in this metaphor than we may realize. We are all familiar, of course, with the truism "You are what you eat." But over the past generation we have learned more and more about the nature of our hungers and how incredibly malleable they are. Scientists and authors like Brian Wansink and Michael Pollan have pointed out how our hungers are *learned*.[1] Of course, *that* we get hungry—that we need to eat—is a structural feature of human biology. But the "direction" our hunger takes—what we hunger *for*—is, in important ways, learned. So it's not just that you are what you eat; you are what you *want* to eat, and this is something that is learned. Your hungers are themselves a kind of habit formed by certain practices. Those hungers, in turn, propel you into routines and rituals that solidify those habits. This is why so much of our eating, as Wansink puts it, is "mindless"—not because we're stupid or ignorant but simply because eating is one of those human activities that is overwhelmingly governed by the power of habit—one of those automaticities described in chapter 2.

Our tastes, as we say, are acquired. But our tastes can be trained without our realizing it. For example, the widespread use of high fructose corn syrup in so many processed food products generates a desire for more of it, despite the negative effects of such processed food products. The result is a vicious circle of hunger that is the product of "engineered" tastes. We learn to crave things that aren't good for us because we are immersed in systems and environments that channel us into this sort of eating. Our hungers are being trained and habituated ("automated") without our realizing it. The same is true for our deepest existential hungers, our *loves*: we might not realize the ways we're being covertly trained to hunger and thirst for idols that can never satisfy.

And here's the real challenge: it turns out you can't just *think* your way to new tastes.

Let me try to make sense of this with an example from my own experience.[2] Over the past several years, through the steady evangelism of my wife, Deanna, I have become more and more convinced about the injustice and unhealthiness of our dominant systems of food production and consumption. For Deanna, this is expressed in a commitment to "good" eating—eating that is both healthy and just, enjoying foods that are the fruit of local gardens and farms, and eating foods that contribute to our flourishing. This finds expression in both her devotion to her gardens and her recruitment of the entire family in a kitchen that is always producing culinary delights (for which I'm incredibly grateful!).

Deanna fills our freezer with what she calls "happy cows" and "happy pigs," animals raised locally in humane environments and even slaughtered in ways that are attentive to their well-being.

Like any obstinate, stiff-necked husband, I was slow to listen and resistant to her arguments. For some reason, it wasn't until I read the same arguments from authors like Barbara Kingsolver and Michael Pollan and especially Wendell Berry that I understood her point. (This frustrating dynamic will no doubt sound familiar to other spouses.) While these authors weren't saying anything Deanna hadn't already told me, when I read her basic argument in Wendell Berry's prose, I was hooked. I was both convicted and convinced. Wendell Berry changed my mind.

But a funny thing happened on the way to the grocery store: I discovered a significant gap between my thought and my action. This hit home to me one day while I was immersed in reading Wendell Berry's delightful anthology *Bringing It to the Table*. For a while, this was my take-with-me book, the book I would keep with me in case I ever had thirty seconds of downtime somewhere. I enthusiastically gobbled up this book, highlighting and underlining and riddling it with checkmarks and "Amen!" affirmations in the margins. As I paused to reflect on a key point, and thus briefly took my nose out of the book, an ugly irony suddenly struck me: I was reading Wendell Berry in the food court at Costco.

There are so many things wrong with that sentence that I don't even know where to begin. Costco, for those who may not know, is a retail chain specializing in big-box, bulk-sized, mass-produced food and other goods. Indeed, "the food court at Costco" might be a kind of shorthand for what Wendell Berry imagines when he pictures the sixth circle of hell. But here I was, munching on one of those Costco footlong hot dogs (almost certainly not from "happy" pigs) while nodding in agreement with Wendell Berry. What was going on?

This was a tangible picture of the gap between what I want and what I *think* I want. More specifically, it clarified the gap between my intellectual convictions and my preintellectual desires, my knowledge and my habits. Obviously I wasn't going to be able to *think* my way to new hungers. New victual knowledge doesn't simply translate into new habits of eating. While Wendell Berry had convinced my intellect, I was still prone to pull into the McDonald's drive-thru. While I *believed* Michael Pollan, that didn't do anything to change the fact that I *wanted* a Big Mac. (Watching the Food Network doesn't make you a gourmet; it doesn't even necessarily make you want what you see.)

You can't just think your way to new hungers. While Pollan and Berry may have successfully recruited my intellect, their books couldn't change my habits. Such rehabituation was going to require a whole new set of practices. And while their arguments could be intellectual catalysts for me—epiphanies of insight into how my hunger-habits had been deformed—*un*learning those habits would require *counter*formative practices, different rhythms and routines that would retrain my hunger. My hungers would have to be retrained so that I would *want* to eat differently. The same is true for our spiritual hungers: new knowledge and information might help me see the power of bad habits, but that in itself is not sufficient to undo them. I can't "know" my way to new habits.

Fast-forward a few years. The arguments and convictions are building up. The sometimes gentle, sometimes not so gentle encouragement from Deanna is becoming more urgent. The scoldings from my doctor are taking on a sharper edge. The nudges from my health insurance company are getting a little more insistent. And something interesting is happening in me: I *want* to want to eat better.

But that desire in itself is not enough to displace a lifetime of hunger-habits that have built up. Those have to be undone and replaced. And that is going to take practice—since that's how I learned the original hungers as well. The way that my hungers have been reformed might be a kind of allegory for our spiritual reformation, I think.

First, in an important sense, I pledged myself to be part of a covenantal community—even if, in this case, it was a "community" consisting only of Deanna and me. Nonetheless, it signals that rehabituation is a communal endeavor precisely because truly (re)formative practices are communal. The basis or platform for the rehabituation of my hungers was a promise Deanna and I made to each other—to encourage one another, to partner in new rhythms, and to keep each other accountable. We would commit together to new rituals of eating and exercise, would partner in cooking and cleanup, would even endure evenings of growling bellies and frustrated sweet tooths *together*. This communal aspect of rehabituation cannot be overemphasized.

Second—perhaps somewhat ironically—in order to reform my wants I would commit myself to practices that I didn't want to do. I submitted myself to new disciplines, apprenticed myself to new regimens of eating and exercise.

I began to exercise, not because I enjoyed it, but because I knew it was good for me. For some reason unbeknownst to me, I decided that running would be the form of exercise I'd adopt. So I laced up my shoes, inserted my ear buds, and started to run toward the river. We live on a hill, so the first half of the run was quite easy; it hadn't occurred to me that I'd have to run back *up* the same hill. For the first few days, my return up that hill was more of a hobble mixed with a dash of waddle. Each day Deanna would ask me, "Did you enjoy that?" "Not for a second," was my reply.

But then one day she asked me the question and I surprised myself by answering, "Yes. That felt good." Eventually I began to realize: I *wanted* to run. And if travel kept me from lacing up my sneakers for a few days, I became antsy and restless, craving a good run. Now I pack my running shoes when I travel and look forward to a run even while I'm on the road. By submitting myself to this exercise regimen, I've basically become a different person: I'm now the guy who *wants* to work out. The practice gave birth to a habit that, in turn, made me *want* the practice and what the practice promises (health, energy, good sleep, emotional stability). I have new cravings. Never could I have imagined that I would *want* to run three miles such that now, even when I'm traveling, I work hard to carve out time to find a treadmill.

Alongside this commitment to regular bodily exercise, I also adopted a new diet, with a little help from Weight Watchers and a lot of help from Deanna. This has become my own little laboratory for understanding rehabituation.

You first need to realize: I was, at best, a "meat and potatoes" guy my whole life—but only if there wasn't any chocolate around. I spent a lifetime eating almost no fruits or vegetables and eating whatever chocolate I could get my hands on. Obviously, something was going to have to change. So I signed up to eat salads and bananas and Greek yogurt while also monitoring the quantity of my intake. This was all facilitated by a smartphone app from Weight Watchers that helped me track what and how much I was eating. While using an app might seem like a very individualist endeavor, in fact it represents the accumulated wisdom of an entire community—of nutritionists and other users who contribute to the shared knowledge available to me in the software. In a sense, the app is the conduit of a community.

Now, on the one hand, the program encourages reflection. It requires you to *think* about what you're eating and drinking all day long. You have to calculate and budget. You have to be conscious of your eating and conscientiously say no. But no one imagines that this kind of conscious, intellectual approach to eating is sustainable over the long haul. Instead, the point of such conscious reflection is precisely to channel you into practices that will, in turn, generate new eating habits. And once those eating habits become automated through repetition, you become a new eater. For the first while, you're like that teenager learning to drive: managing your eating with that snowball on the tip of the iceberg of consciousness, *thinking* about everything, but in fact that is just the entrée into a way of life where your habits change your hungers.[3]

Spiritual formation in Christ requires a lot of *re*habituation precisely because we build up so many disordered habits over a lifetime. This is also why the spiritual formation of children is one of the most significant callings of the body of Christ. Every child raised in the church and in a Christian home has the opportunity to be immersed in kingdom-indexed habit-forming practices from birth. This is why intentionality about the formation of children is itself a gift of the Spirit. It's also why carelessness and inattention to the deformative power of cultural liturgies can have such long-lasting effects. The "plasticity" of children's habits and imaginations is an opportunity and a challenge.

For a tangible expression of this, see Destin Sandlin's remarkable video, "The Backwards Brain Bicycle."[a] Sandlin creates a bicycle with an important hitch: when you turn the handlebars left, the front wheel turns right—and vice versa. Having ridden a bike his entire life, Sandlin literally cannot ride this bike. His neural pathways and bodily habits are trained for a regular bicycle. His "habituations" are very settled. Only with extraordinary effort does Sandlin learn to ride the bike—after eight months of practice! **Old habits die hard.**

But the story was very different for Sandlin's son: he learned to ride the "backwards bike" in just two weeks. There is an important spiritual insight here: families and churches should not just be focused on informing young minds; they should be looking to form habits early on.

a. http://bit.ly/BackwardsBike.

The result? I have new hungers. Never could I have imagined that I would *crave* a salad or have a hankering for Greek yogurt or—even more miraculously—say no to chocolate. The rituals changed my habits, which in turn generated new (rightly ordered) hungers. I went from being someone who wanted to want the right things to someone who—not always, but more often than not—now wants them and acts accordingly.

I hope the upshot of this analogy is fairly obvious. If love is both habit and hunger, then our tastes and cravings for what's ultimate will be changed in the same way. Reflection is important—indeed,

I hope this book can serve as a catalyst for your *thinking about* the liturgical formation (and deformation) of your loves. But reflection should propel us into new practices that will reform our hungers by inscribing new habits.

The church—the body of Christ—is the place where God invites us to renew our loves, reorient our desires, and retrain our appetites. Indeed, isn't the church where we are nourished by the Word, where we "eat the Word" and receive the bread of life? The church is that household where the Spirit feeds us what we need and where, by his grace, we become a people who desire him above all else. Christian worship is the feast where we acquire new hungers—for God and for what God desires—and are then sent into his creation to act accordingly.

But the practices of the church are also a spiritual workout, inviting us into routines that train our heart muscles, our fundamental desires that govern how we move and act in the world. As Matthew Boulton notes, this metaphor is at least as old as John Calvin: "For Calvin, the church is a gymnasium, a training ground, a school, and community of preparation and practice enrolled (we hope and pray) in God's sanctifying, transformative *paideia*."[4]

Our sanctification—the process of becoming holy and Christlike—is more like a Weight Watchers program than listening to a book on tape. If sanctification is tantamount to closing the gap between what I know and what I do (no longer reading Wendell Berry in Costco, essentially), it means changing what I want. And that requires submitting ourselves to disciplines and regimens that reach down into our deepest habits. The Spirit of God meets us in that space—in that gap—not with lightning bolts of magic but with the concrete practices of the body of Christ that conscript our bodily habits. If we think of sanctification as learning to "put on" or "clothe" ourselves with Christ (Rom. 13:14; Col. 3:14), this is intimately bound up with becoming in*corp*orated into his body, the *corpus Christi*.

Discipleship is a kind of immigration, from the kingdom of darkness to the kingdom of God's beloved Son (Col. 1:13). In Christ we are given a heavenly passport; in his body we learn how to live like "locals" of his kingdom. Such an immigration to a new kingdom isn't just a matter of being teleported to a different realm; we need to be acclimated to a new way of life, learn a new language, acquire new habits—and unlearn the habits of that rival dominion. Christian worship is our enculturation as citizens of heaven, subjects of kingdom come (Phil. 3:20).

Habitations of the Spirit

There's an old preacher's joke you've perhaps heard before. A village faces rising floodwaters. In town is a devout Christian man who fervently knows that God is going to save him from this calamity. He is convinced that God will come to his aid.

When the waters rise to his knees and his neighbors are making their way out of town in rowboats, friends in a canoe paddle by and urge him, "Jump in! We're here to save you." "No, no, I'll be fine," the man replies. "God is going to save me." Puzzled, the friends in the canoe paddle on.

The waters continue to climb, pouring through windows. Our devout Christian man, perplexed but still fervent in his expectation, is treading water in his living room when a motorboat speeds up. "C'mon! Get in!" his would-be rescuers shout. "We're here to save you!" "Don't worry about it," the man says, winded from paddling. "I'm fine. *God* is going to save me." The boaters insist, but to no avail.

Finally, the man has to climb on top of his roof. Dark, surging waters have overwhelmed the eaves. The village is quiet. Cold, befuddled, trying his best to quell his doubts, the man is sitting on the peak of the house when he hears the thud-thud-thud of a helicopter in the distance. Making its way toward him, its roar gets closer and closer until he realizes they've come for him. The

Coast Guard chopper lowers a basket, and a rescue diver shouts over the whir of the blades, "Climb in, sir! It's alright! We're here to save you!" You won't be surprised by the man's response: he refuses, citing once again his confidence that God is going to save him. The diver tries hard to convince him, but it's no use. The chopper chugs away without its intended passenger.

The story comes to a tragic end. In heaven, the bewildered man respectfully says to the Lord, "I thought you were going to save me. Where were you?"

"What are you talking about?" the Lord replies. "I sent a canoe, a boat, and a helicopter. What more did you want?"

The story, while quaint, gets at an important truth: too often we look for the Spirit in the extraordinary when God has promised to be present in the ordinary.[5] We look for God in the fresh and novel, as if his grace were always an "event," when he has promised that his Spirit faithfully attends the ordinary means of grace—in the Word, at the Table. We keep looking for God in the new, as if grace were always bound up with "the next best thing," but Jesus encouraged us to look for God in a simple, regular meal.

More concretely, the story illustrates an incarnational lesson: God meets us where we are. While we might be expecting some remarkable, unmistakably divine mode of interaction, God shows

> Michael Horton notes our penchant for the extraordinary, which means we end up ignoring the ordinary means of grace right in front of us.
>
> American Christianity is a story of perpetual upheavals in churches and individual lives. Starting with the extraordinary conversion experience, our lives are motivated by a constant expectation for The Next Big Thing. We're growing bored with **the ordinary means of God's grace**, attending church week in and week out. Doctrines and disciplines that have shaped faithful Christian witness in the past are often marginalized or substituted with newer fashions or methods. The new and improved may dazzles us for a moment, but soon they have become "so last year."[a]
>
> a. Michael Horton, *Ordinary: Sustainable Faith in a Radical, Restless World* (Grand Rapids: Zondervan, 2014), 16.

up at our flooding house with a canoe, a boat, a helicopter. In a similar way, the Lord knows that we are creatures of habit; he created us this way. God knows that we are animated by hungers we aren't always aware of, that our wants and cravings are inscribed in us by habit-forming practices that teach us to want. If you are a creature of habit whose loves have been deformed by disordered secular liturgies, then the best gift God could give you is Spirit-infused practices that will reform and retrain your loves. And so he meets us where we are, with counterformative practices, with hunger-shaping rituals and love-shaping liturgies. He gives us Spirit-empowered practices as the gifts of God for the people of God. This is what Dallas Willard means when he talks about "the Spirit *of* the disciplines"—that the spiritual disciplines are conduits of the Spirit's transforming grace.[6] I want to supplement Willard's emphasis on the individual practice of the spiritual disciplines with what might be a counterintuitive thesis in our "millennial" moment: that the most potent, charged, transformative site of the Spirit's work is found in the most unlikely of places—the church!

I don't have a radical thesis to offer about discipleship. You won't find in this book some new program or novel formula, some previously unknown secret revealed by a guru who finally solves the problem of discipleship—like the spiritual equivalent of those weight-loss pills you see advertised on television (if only!). To the contrary, my argument is the very opposite of novel; it's ancient: the church's worship is the heart of discipleship. Yes, Christian formation is a life-encompassing, Monday through Saturday, week in and week out project; but it radiates from, and is nourished by, the worship life of the congregation gathered around Word and Table. There is no sanctification without the church, not because some building holds a superstitious magic, but rather because the church is the very body of Christ, animated by the Spirit of God and composed of Spirited practices. As Craig Dykstra once put it, "The life of Christian faith is the practice of many practices," not because this is something *we* accomplish, but because these practices are the "habitations of the Spirit."[7] The practices of prayer and song, preaching and offering, baptism and Communion, are the canoes and boats and helicopters that God graciously sends our way. He meets us where we are, as creatures of habit who are shaped by practices, and invites us into a community of practice that is the very *body* of his Son. Liturgy is the way we learn to "put on" Christ (Col. 3:12–16).

Whose Worship? Who's Acting?

Unfortunately, the notion that worship is the heart of discipleship is liable to misunderstanding because our working definition of worship has become so narrow and reductionistic. When we hear the word "worship," 90 percent of us probably think of "music" or the "song service" that precedes the sermon ("teaching"). As a result, we also tend to primarily think of worship as something *we* do. So if we are going to properly understand how and why worship is the heart of discipleship, we need to stretch, expand, and, frankly, correct our understanding of worship. In doing so, we will remember wisdom the church has forgotten in modernity. In this sense, I hope you might find a sense of liberation by embracing liturgy.

For some of us, especially those of us who are Protestant evangelicals, "liturgy" is going to sound like a bad word. It's loaded with connotations that make us suspicious: it sounds like "vain repetition," the dread "religion" that is an expression of human effort. In short, we might react to "liturgy" as if the very notion is bound up with salvation by works, salvation by ritual observance.

What's interesting is that the Protestant Reformers had exactly those kinds of reservations about medieval Roman Catholic worship. But their response, rather than being *anti*liturgical, was to be *properly* liturgical. The problem wasn't liturgy per se, but disordered liturgies. In particular, the Reformers were critical of worship practices that had been effectively "naturalized"—forms of worship that construed liturgical practices as operations of merely human effort. This is a temptation of any form of worship that takes the body seriously—to naturalize the liturgy as *just* an embodied practice like any other, as if the formation of disciples in Christian worship operates in pretty much the same way as the formation of José Bautista as an excellent hitter through bodily rituals of batting practice. While worship is entirely embodied, it is not *only* material; and though worship is wholly natural, it is never *only* natural. Christian worship is nothing less than an invitation to participate in the life of the Triune God. In short, the centrality of embodiment should not be understood as a naturalizing of worship that would deny the dynamic presence of the Spirit. To the contrary, the Spirit meets, nourishes, transforms, and empowers us just *through* and *in* such material practices. The church's worship is a uniquely intense site of the Spirit's transformative presence. As Marva Dawn has put it, God is both the subject and the object of our worship. The whole point of "liturgical lines and rituals" is to create "a powerful environment of God-centeredness."[8] Worship is not *for me*—it's not primarily meant to be an experience that "meets my felt needs," nor should we reduce it to merely a pedagogy of desire (which would be just a more sophisticated *pro me* construal of worship); rather, worship is about and for God. To say that God is both subject and object is to emphasize that the Triune God is both the audience and the agent of worship: worship is *to* and *for* God, and God is active *in* worship in the Word and the sacraments.

This is where the Reformers' sense of liturgical reform has contemporary relevance. As Nicholas Wolterstorff has pointed out, the medieval Western liturgy against which the Reformers reacted was beset by its own kind of "naturalization" insofar as it "was a liturgy in which, to an extraordinary degree, the action of God was lost from view. The actions were all human. The priest addressed God. The priest brought about Christ's bodily, but static, presence. . . . But God as agent is nowhere in view."[9] If there was any concern with action, it was focused on the "work of the people," the upward acts of expression and ritual observance that, ironically, were only really carried out by human beings.

In contrast, it is an emphasis on action, and particularly *God's* action in worship, that Wolterstorff distills as the "genius" of Reformed and Protestant worship. "The liturgy as the Reformers understood and practiced it consists of God acting and us responding through the work of the Spirit." As such,

> the Reformers saw the liturgy as *God's action and our faithful reception of that action*. The governing idea of the Reformed liturgy is thus twofold: the conviction that to participate in the liturgy is to enter the sphere of God's acting, not just of God's presence, plus the conviction that we are to appropriate God's action in faith and gratitude through the work of the Spirit. . . . The liturgy is a meeting between God and God's people, a meeting in which both parties act, but in which God initiates and we respond.[10]

Thus Calvin emphasized that the sacraments "are not strictly the works of men but of God. In Baptism or the Lord's Supper we do nothing; we simply come to God to receive His grace. Baptism, from our side, is a passive work. We bring nothing to it but faith, which has all things laid up in Christ."[11] Reformed liturgical theologian Hughes Oliphant Old captures this well when he argues, "What Calvin has in mind is that God is active in our worship. When we worship God according to his Word, he is at work in the worship of the church. For Calvin the worship of the church is a matter of divine activity rather than human creativity."[12]

So worship is a site of God's action, not just God's presence. The emphasis—in accordance with Calvin's theology of grace— is on the primacy of God's gracious initiation. *God* is the first and primary actor in worship. But the point isn't passivity, turning us into a mere audience, spectators of what Someone Else is doing (that was the problem with medieval worship!). Instead, this emphasis on God's action in worship includes a picture of graced *inter*action between God and his people, a liturgical form

Zairon / Wikimedia Commons

"The worship of the church is a matter of divine activity rather than human creativity" (Hughes Oliphant Old).

of call and response, grace and gratitude. Wolterstorff sees this highlighted in the liturgical theology of a later Calvinist, Dutch theologian Abraham Kuyper. Commenting on Kuyper's proposals for liturgical reform, Wolterstorff observes that, for Kuyper, "various parts of the liturgy, and the liturgy as a whole, are to

be seen as 'an *interaction between God and the congregation.*'
Liturgy is action; and the actions are not just human actions and
not just divine actions but 'an interaction between God and his
people, in which the congregation self-consciously participates.'"[13]
But this shouldn't be confused with a liturgical Pelagianism
that places a priority on human effort, precisely because even such
*inter*action is made possible by trinitarian operations of grace.
Worship, as Philip Butin puts it, is a "trinitarian enactment" in
which "the initiatory 'downward' movement of Christian worship
begins in the Father's gracious and free revelation of the divine
nature to the church through the Son, by means of the Spirit. . . .
The 'upward' movement of human response in worship . . . is
also fundamentally motivated by God. Human response—'the
sacrifice of praise and thanksgiving'—arises from the faith that
has its source in the indwelling Holy Spirit."[14] For the Reformers,
even our "expression" of gratitude is made possible by the gracious work of the Spirit. This is liturgical theology that expresses
the mystery and good news of Ephesians 2:8–10.

Let's return from the Reformation to our contemporary context:
Might these historical insights about liturgical renewal be relevant
today? Do we need another reformation of our worship? Has contemporary evangelical worship ended up—ironically—mimicking
the scripted naturalism and spectatorish passivity that occasioned
the Protestant Reformation? In what ways do our current patterns
of "contemporary worship" effectively make *us* the only "actors"
in worship—not only failing to appreciate the *primacy* of God's
action in worship but failing even to see God as active in our worship? Have we not fallen prey once again to the static medieval
paradigm that is focused on "presence"?

One Sunday I undertook a little exercise with my daughter while
in the pew. Our congregation usually sang from a hymnbook, but
on this Sunday we sang a contemporary praise chorus that was
printed in our bulletin. I invited her to see the implicit theology
of the song through a grammatical analysis. I handed her a pencil

with two simple instructions: draw a circle around every use of "me" or "I" and draw a square around every reference to God or Christ, and then let's compare the two.

You can imagine which of the two categories won. I don't mean to disparage the contemporary per se, nor do I mean to suggest that the age of a hymn makes it immune to bad theology. I simply invite us to recognize that the very form of our songs, in their grammatical structure, can implicitly say—and hence teach us— something about *who* we think is active in worship. And when our songs attribute the action of worship to *us* ("Here *I* am to worship, here *I* am to bow down . . ."), then worship is understood as fundamentally an expression of human will, a Pelagian endeavor of self-assertion. If that's how we tacitly think of worship, then the claim that worship is the heart of discipleship will seem odd.

But if we recover a sense of the primacy of God's action in worship—that worship is a site of gracious, divine initiative—then we might better understand how and why worship is the center of discipleship. We should approach the sanctuary with a different set of expectations—that we will be met and remade by a living, active Lord.

From Expression to Formation

Our sense of who is active in worship should fundamentally challenge another widespread misconception that probably also taints how we hear the word "worship." When we tacitly assume that *we* are the primary actors in worship, then we also assume that worship is basically an *expressive* endeavor. This is why we now constrict "worship" to the song service of our gathering, the time in the service when we can express ourselves. We think of worship primarily in a bottom-up framework, as a way for us to express our praise and show our devotion—as if worship gathers us to perform for God as our proverbial "audience of one." When we think of worship in this way, then we also assume that the most important characteristic of our worship is that it should be *sincere*. If worship is expression of our devotion to God, then the last thing we want to be is a hypocrite: our expression needs to be honest, true, fresh, genuine, "authentic."

But this creates an interesting challenge because sincerity and authenticity tend to generate a penchant for *novelty*. If I worship in order to show God how much I love him, I might start to feel hypocritical if I just keep doing the same thing over and over and over again. My expression will start to feel less "authentic." And so we need to find new ways to worship, new ways to show our devotion, fresh new forms to express our praise. Novelty is how we try to maintain the fresh sincerity of worship that is fundamentally understood as expression.

With the best of intentions, this "expressive" paradigm is then allied to a questionable distinction between the form of worship and the content of the gospel. The concrete shape and practices of Christian worship, passed down through the centuries, are considered merely optional forms—or even whited sepulchers of dead ritual—that can and should be discarded in order to communicate the gospel "message" in ways that are contemporary, attractive, and relevant. So we remake the church in order to "speak to" contemporary culture.

In our desire to embed the gospel content in forms that are attractional, accessible, and not off-putting, we look around for contemporary cultural forms that are more familiar. Instead of asking contemporary seekers and Christians to inhabit old, stodgy medieval practices that are foreign and strange, we retool worship by adopting contemporary practices that can be easily entered precisely because they are so familiar. Rather than the daunting, spooky ambience of the Gothic cathedral, we invite people to worship in the ethos of the coffee shop, the concert, or the mall. Confident in the form/content distinction, we believe we can distill the gospel content and embed it in these new forms, since the various practices are effectively neutral: just temporal containers for an eternal message. We distill "Jesus" out of the inherited, ancient forms of historic worship (which we'll discard as "traditional") in order to present Jesus in forms that are both fresh and familiar: come meet Jesus in the sanctified experience of a coffee shop; come hear the gospel in a place that should feel familiar since we've modeled it after the mall.

The problem, of course, is that these "forms" are not just neutral containers or discardable conduits for a message. As we've seen already, what are embraced as merely fresh forms are, in fact, *practices* that are already oriented to a certain *telos*, a tacit vision of the good life. Indeed, I've tried to show that these cultural practices are *liturgies* in their own right precisely because they are oriented to a *telos* and are bent on shaping my loves and longings. The forms themselves are pedagogies of desire that teach us to construe and relate to the world in a loaded way. So when we distill the gospel message and embed it in the form of the mall, while we might think we are finding a fresh way for people to encounter Christ, in fact the very form of the practice is already loaded with a way of construing the world. The liturgy of the mall is a heart-level education in consumerism that construes everything as a commodity available to make me happy. When I encounter "Jesus" in such a liturgy, rather than encountering the living Lord of history, I am implicitly being taught that Jesus is one more commodity available to make me happy. And while I might eagerly want to add him to my shelf of stuff, we shouldn't confuse this appropriation with discipleship.

This bottom-up paradigm of worship as expression characterizes much of what we immediately picture when we think of worship, particularly in North American evangelicalism (google "worship" and look at the images: you'll see what I mean). It's also why so many are suspicious of "liturgy." If you think of worship as expressive, you'll tend to confuse ritual with "works righteousness"; that is, you will look at "liturgical" worship—Christian worship that reflects ancient forms and practices—as insincere ways that people try to "earn" God's favor.

But that is to look at liturgical forms of worship from an expressivist paradigm they don't share. Expressivists assume theirs is the only way to understand worship, and so they impose their expressivism on historic Christian worship and see only insincerity and rote repetition. But the irony is that this stems from the fact that the worship-as-expression paradigm makes *us* the primary actors in worship. In other words, expressivism breeds its own kind of bottom-up valorization of human striving that slides closer to works righteousness.

But the practices of historic Christian worship are not just old, "traditional" ways that Christians gathered around Word and Table. They are rooted in a fundamentally different understanding of what worship is, a fundamentally different paradigm of the primary *agent* of Christian worship. Instead of the bottom-up emphasis on worship as *our* expression of devotion and praise, historic Christian worship is rooted in the conviction that God is the primary actor or agent in the worship encounter. Worship works from the top down, you might say. In worship we don't just come to show God our devotion and give him our praise; we are called to worship because in this encounter God (re)makes and molds us top-down. Worship is the arena in which God recalibrates our hearts, reforms our desires, and rehabituates our loves. Worship isn't just something we do; it is where God does something *to* us. Worship is the heart of discipleship because it is the gymnasium in which God retrains our hearts.

Form Matters

This engenders a counterintuitive hypothesis: to the extent that we recover a biblical sense of the primacy of God's action in worship, we will also recover an appreciation for why the *form* of worship matters. I call this "counterintuitive" because I think we probably associate liturgical formalism with the sort of ritualism that the Reformers were calling into question. But it is precisely because we have a deep sense of God's trinitarian agency and action in worship that we need to be attentive to—and intentional about—the form of our worship, and particularly how the Spirit gifts us with forms of worship that meet us as the embodied creatures we are. When we realize that worship is also about *form*ation, we will begin to appreciate why *form* matters. The practices we submit ourselves to in Christian worship are God's way of rehabituating our loves toward the kingdom, so we need to be intentional about the Story that is carried in those practices.

By the "form" of worship I mean two things: (1) the overall narrative arc of a service of Christian worship and (2) the concrete, received practices that constitute elements of that enacted narrative. Formative Christian worship has an intentional, biblical *shape* about it as a nexus of practices that recalibrates our hearts toward God and his kingdom. In the next chapter we'll look in more detail at the way historic Christian worship invites us into the Story of God in Christ reconciling the world to himself (2 Cor. 5:19). Here I simply want to make a broader point: worship is not primarily a venue for innovative creativity but a place for discerning reception and faithful repetition. That doesn't mean there's no room for faithful innovation in worship; it just means that creativity and novelty in worship are not goods in and of themselves. We inherit a form of worship that should be received as a gift.

I'm not talking about the "style" of worship. While the form/style distinction is itself somewhat tenuous, let me at least say that when I'm speaking about the form of intentional, historic Christian worship, I'm *not* making a case for "traditional" worship versus "contemporary" worship. I'm not arguing for pipe organs over guitars or taking sides in a choirs-versus-drums debate. Musical styles are their own sorts of forms, to be sure, but that's not what I mean here.[15]

My point is at once more fundamental and less nostalgic: Christian worship is the heart of discipleship just to the extent that it is a repertoire of practices shaped by the biblical story. Only worship that is oriented by the biblical story and suffused with the Spirit will be a *counter*formative practice that can undo the habituations of rival, secular liturgies. Not everything that calls itself "worship" today will have this counterformative power, since so many of our worship services are little more than Jesufied versions of secular liturgies. They claim the name of worship but deny the power thereof. So while we may be singing songs about Jesus, the very shape or form of the worship "experience" in fact reinforces the gospel of consumerism and the unwitting encounter with Jesus as simply one more commodity. The story carried in such contemporary forms of worship is one whose *telos* is not God's vision of *shalom* but consumerism's vision of happiness via consumption and disposal.

This is why those of us who inhabit postmodernity have so much to learn from ancient Christians. Because the rituals and liturgies of their surrounding culture were much more overt—for example, their civic political spaces were unabashedly temples, whereas ours traffic under euphemisms (stadiums, capitols, universities)—early Christians were more intentional about and conscious of the practices they adopted for worship. The heart and soul of their liturgical life hearkened back to Israel, but they didn't simply "Jesufy" the synagogue. There was faithful innovation as the disciples sought to discern the rhythms and practices that would constitute the community of Christ. This included responding specifically to Jesus's commands (giving us baptism and the Lord's Supper, for example), but it also included careful selection, reappropriation, and reorientation of formative cultural practices into the repertoire of kingdom-indexed liturgy. Thus, over time, the body of Christ continued to discern the scripts that should characterize a worshiping community centered on the ascended Christ who prayed for kingdom come.

The result is a rich legacy of worship wisdom that can be inherited by all Christians as a repertoire for faith formation. This is why we can say that the shape of historic, intentional, formative

Christian worship is "catholic"—not because it is "Roman" but because the repertoire of historic Christian worship represents the accumulated wisdom of the body of Christ led by the Spirit into truth, as Jesus promised (John 16:13). Let's not imagine that this is only a promise about doctrinal correctness; it is also a promise that the same Spirit would lead the body of Christ to discern a way of life that is faithful. In chapter 4 we'll look at the plotline of such formative worship and consider some of the "stage directions" that accompany it. But it's important for us to see this liturgical heritage as an expression of our catholic faith—the common, orthodox heritage of the church that is shared across an array of Christian traditions, just like the Nicene Creed. When our worship has a common form it reinforces our oneness and unity, which is especially important for the church's witness in our post-Christian age.

If worship is formative, not merely expressive, then we need to be conscious and intentional about the form of worship that is forming us. This has one more important implication: When you unhook worship from mere expression, it also completely retools your understanding of *repetition*. If you think of worship as a bottom-up, expressive endeavor, repetition will seem insincere and inauthentic. But when you see worship as an invitation to a top-down encounter in which God is refashioning your deepest habits, then repetition looks very different: it's how God rehabituates us. In a formational paradigm, repetition isn't insincere, because you're not *showing*, you're *submitting*. This is crucial because there is no formation without repetition. Virtue formation takes practice, and there is no practice that isn't repetitive. We willingly embrace repetition as a good in all kinds of other sectors of our life—to hone our golf swing, our piano prowess, and our mathematical abilities, for example. If the sovereign Lord has created us as creatures of habit, why should we think repetition is inimical to our spiritual growth?

Oscar Wilde's provocative dialogue "The Critic as Artist" articulates a relevant insight for us here: learning to love takes practice, and practice takes repetition. In some ways, we belong *in order* to believe. "Do you wish to love?" Gilbert asks in the dialogue. "Use Love's Litany, and the words will create the yearning from which the world fancies they spring."[16] The liturgy of Christian worship is the litany of love we pray over and over again, given to us by the Spirit precisely in order to cultivate the love he sheds abroad in our hearts.

4

WHAT STORY ARE YOU IN?

The Narrative Arc of Formative Christian Worship

Understanding the Gospel with Your Gut

Worship is the heart of discipleship if and only if worship is a repertoire of Spirit-endued practices that grab hold of your gut, recalibrate your *kardia*, and capture your imagination. Because we are liturgical animals, we need to recognize the rival liturgies that vie for our hearts and then commit ourselves to the rightly ordered liturgy of Christian worship as a recalibration and rehabituation project. And if you are someone responsible for leading the people of God in worship, the implications are further ramped up: every pastor is a curate and every elder a curator, responsible for the care of souls and responsible to curate hearts by planning and leading worship that undertakes this formative task.

You won't be liberated from *de*formation by new *in*formation. God doesn't deliver us from the deformative habit-forming power of tactile rival liturgies by merely giving us a book. Instead, he invites us into a different embodied liturgy that not only is suffused by the biblical story but also, via those practices, inscribes the story into our hearts as our erotic calibration, bending the needle of our loves toward Christ, our magnetic north. The Scriptures seep into us in a unique way in the intentional, communal rituals of worship. If we want to be a people oriented by a biblical worldview and guided by biblical wisdom, one of the best spiritual investments we can make is to mine the riches of historic Christian worship, which is rooted in the conviction that the Word is caught more than it is taught. The drama of redemption told in the Scriptures is enacted in worship in a way that makes it "sticky."[1] Study and memorization are important, but there is a unique, imagination-forming power in the communal, repeated, and poetic cadences of historic Christian worship.

Alan Jacobs masterfully rehearses how this combination of convictions—that Christian worship should be, first and foremost, biblical and that the Word seeps into us through ritual—informed Thomas Cranmer's creation of the Book of Common Prayer. Far from being antithetical to liturgy, it was Cranmer's evangelical conviction about the centrality of the Bible to the Christian life that propelled his creation of the rites of the prayer book.[2] This included the regularization of "the Kalendar"—a regimen of public reading, akin to what we now call the lectionary, that would take the people of God through the whole of the Scriptures on a regular basis and through the entirety of the Psalms (the church's ancient hymnbook) each month. But in addition to the prescribed rhythm of Scripture readings, Cranmer's prayers were also drenched in biblical language and were another way that English Christians would absorb a biblical sensibility on a subconscious register. Jacobs cites Eamon Duffy's grudging admission of the impact of the Book of Common Prayer: "Cranmer's sombrely magnificent prose, read week by week, entered and possessed their minds, and became the fabric of their prayer, the utterance of their most solemn and their most vulnerable moments."[3] And insofar as

Cranmer's prose was really a deployment of the language of the Scriptures, the rites and rituals of the Book of Common Prayer dug wells into the very imagination of those who prayed according to its cadences.[4]

To be conformed to the image of his Son is not only to think God's thoughts after him but to desire what God desires. That requires the recalibration of our heart-habits and the recapturing of our imagination, which happens when God's Word becomes the orienting center of our social imaginary, shaping our very perception of things before we even *think* about them. So, like the secular liturgies of the mall or the stadium or the frat house, Christian liturgies can't just target the intellect: they also work on the body, conscripting our desires through the senses. Christian worship that will be counterformative needs to be embodied, tangible, and visceral. The way to the heart is through the body. That's why counterformative Christian worship doesn't just dispense information; rather, it is a Christ-centered imagination station where we regularly undergo a ritual cleansing of the symbolic universes we absorb elsewhere. Christian worship doesn't just teach us how to think; it teaches us how to love, and it does so by inviting us into the biblical story and implanting that story in our bones.

A quip often attributed to Mark Twain gets at this: "He who carries a cat by the tail learns something he can learn in no other way." Think about that for a second. Imagine I've carried a cat by the tail before. Imagine I am a master explainer who can describe to you what that experience was like in evocative, concrete ways. Hearing my account will *never* be the same as actually carrying a cat by the tail. Why? Because there is an irreducible know-how "carried" in the experience itself. There is something about this reality that I can only know in the practice itself. I learn something in the doing that can't ever be put into words and yet is its own irreducible sort of understanding.

So too in the rhythms and cadences of full-orbed Christian worship, we learn something about the gospel that we couldn't learn

in any other way—and might not even be able to put into words.
Carried in the practices of Christian worship is an understanding
of God that we "know" on a register deeper than the intellect,
an understanding of the gospel on the level of the imagination
that changes how we comport ourselves in the world, even if we
can never quite articulate it in beliefs or doctrines or a Christian
worldview.

In this chapter we'll consider the plot and practices of historic
Christian worship as gifts of the tradition handed down to us for
our (re)formation.

Worship Character-izes Us

Every liturgy, we've said, is oriented toward a *telos*—an implicit
vision of flourishing that is loaded into its rituals. Those formed
by such liturgies then become the kind of people who pursue and
desire that end. So if we are unreflectively immersed in the liturgies
of consumerism, we will, over time, "learn" that the end goal of
human life is acquisition and consumption. "What is the chief end
of man?" the consumerist catechism asks. "To acquire stuff with
the illusion that I can enjoy it forever." Or, if we are immersed in
what Augustine describes as the "civic rituals" of various outposts
of the "earthly city," we will be formed to pursue domination as
our *telos* and to live accordingly.

Christian worship comes loaded with its own vision of flourishing, one that is not just "spiritual" or ethereal or displaced to
a disembodied heaven. The biblical vision of creation's *shalom* is
"heavenly," but it envisions a heavenly order that becomes a reality
on earth (Rev. 21:1–2). This is a *telos* we learn in prayer: "your
kingdom come, your will be done, on earth as it is in heaven"
(Matt. 6:10). This is not an escapist vision but a reparative one:
God is not going to destroy all things but will *renew* all things.
Thus the biblical vision of our *telos* is, as we've said above, a
kind of sanctified humanism—a vision of how to be human.

The biblical vision refuses any dichotomy between the natural and the supernatural. Rather, as Henri de Lubac put it, humanity is created with a natural desire for the supernatural, and the supernatural operations of grace enable us to realize the natural ends for which we were created.[5] N. T. Wright captures well this resonance between the natural and the supernatural in biblical Christianity:

> The Christian vision of virtue, of character that has become second nature, is precisely all about discovering what it means to be truly human—human in a way most of us never imagine. And if that is so, there are bound to be overlaps with other human visions of virtue, as well as points at which Christianity issues quite different demands and offers quite different help in meeting them. Part of the claim of the early Christians, in fact, was that in and through Jesus they had discovered *both* a totally different way of being human *and* a way which scooped up the best that ancient wisdom had to offer and placed it in a framework where it could, at last, make sense. The New Testament itself continually points to this.[6]

In Christ, the image of the invisible God (Col. 1:15), we become the image bearers we were created to be (Gen. 1:27–30). In ways that echo Augustine's "design" claim for human nature, Wright continues:

> What are we here for in the first place? The fundamental answer . . . is that what we're "here for" is to become genuine human beings, reflecting the God in whose image we're made, and doing so in worship on the one hand and in mission, its full and large sense, on the other; and that we do this not least by "following Jesus." The way this works out is that it produces, through the work of the Holy Spirit, a transformation of character. This transformation will mean that we do indeed "keep the rules"—though not out of a sense of externally imposed "duty," but out of character that has been formed within us. And it will mean that we do indeed "follow our hearts" and live "authentically"—but only when, with that transformed character fully operative (like an airline pilot with a lifetime's experience), the hard work up front bears fruit in spontaneous decisions and actions that

reflect what has been formed deep within. And, in the wider world, the
challenge we face is to grow and develop a fresh generation of leaders,
in all walks of life, whose character has been formed in wisdom and
public service, not in greed for money or power.[7]

"What are we here for?" Wright asks. The question has a cosmic
scope and a congregational implication. On the one hand, this is
one of those ultimate queries, one of those "big questions" that
uniquely besets human beings: What is the meaning of it all?
What's the point? What is our purpose in life? What are we here
for? On the other hand, this is also a question that can be asked
of worship, a question that can burble up for us as we walk down
the aisle to our pew or as we fidget during the organ's prelude:
What are we here for? What's the point? What is the purpose of
worship?

Interestingly, Wright's answer is the same for both questions:
"What we're 'here for' is to become genuine human beings, reflecting the God in whose image we're made." The end of worship is
bound up with the end of being human. In other words, the point
of *worship* is bound up with the point of *creation*. The goal of
Christian worship is a renewal of the mandate in creation: to be
(re)made in God's image and then *sent* as his image bearers *to*
and *for* the world.

Another way of getting at this is to say that one of the goals
of Christian worship is to "character-ize" us, in a twofold sense.
First, as we've already seen, Wright invites us to see Scripture as
the narration of the unfolding drama of the God who acts. We are
called to be characters in this story, to play the role of God's image
bearers who care for and cultivate God's creation, to the praise
of his glory. To learn this role is to become what we were made
to be. This is not playacting or pretending: it is the role we were
born to play. In becoming these characters, we become ourselves.
To assume this role is to find our vocation. The dynamics here are
similar to the dynamics of Augustine's *Confessions*, which opens
with his famous prayer: "You have made us for yourself, and our

heart is restless until it rests in you." Augustine spends a lifetime looking for love in all the wrong places, trying on roles and playing characters that dehumanize him and take him further and further from the Creator. Not until he "puts on" Christ does he find himself, becoming who he was made to be. Only then does he assume the character he was made to play.

But Christian worship also "character-izes" us in a second sense: in the rhythms of worship, the Spirit inscribes in us the *character* that makes us a certain kind of person. How are these two senses of "character-ization" connected? What does becoming a character in God's drama have to do with acquiring the character that reflects virtue? In his important book *After Virtue*, Alasdair MacIntyre famously says, "I cannot answer the question, 'What ought I to do?' unless I first answer the question, 'Of which story am I a part?'"[8] We're now in a place to appreciate this point anew: it is the story of which I'm a part—in which I'm a character—that determines just what counts as character, as virtue.

What counts as a virtue is relative to a goal or an end that is envisioned, a *telos*. If a habit is a disposition toward a certain *telos*, an inclination to act in a certain "direction," then we need to determine the *telos* in order to be able to determine whether a habit is a virtue or a vice. So to know whether a habit is a virtue or a vice, we need to answer Wright's question: "What are we here for?"

This is why virtue is bound up with a sense of excellence: a virtue is a disposition that inclines us to achieve the good for which we are made. In other words, a virtue is a good habit that inclines us toward the *telos* that is best for us. Not unless we specify that *end* can we know whether something or someone is functioning well. Take a nonmoral example: Let's say I have a flute and I'm using it to roast marshmallows over a campfire (it's a long story—don't ask). As you can imagine, it doesn't work out very well, and I throw down the instrument in frustration. "This is a terrible flute!" I say. Well, no, not really, because I'm not using it for what it was made for. Roasting marshmallows is not the proper *telos* for a flute.

You can see how deep disagreements about the *telos* of humanity could generate radically different accounts of what is virtuous and what is vicious. But we often don't articulate these different ends. They remain largely implicit—yet deeply influential—in different narratives (different worldviews or social imaginaries, you might say) that envision very different *ends* for humanity. For example, a narrative or worldview that values power and domination and violence will see Christ's meekness and humility as a vice; in contrast, Christians see Christ as the very exemplar of virtue, and so we evaluate his meekness and humility as virtues to which we aspire.

Indeed, the *telos* for Christians *is* Christ: Jesus Christ is the very embodiment of what we're made for, of the end to which we are called. This is why Paul's exhortation to "put on love" (Col. 3:14) is equivalent to the exhortation to "put on the Lord Jesus Christ" (Rom. 13:14 NRSV). This is how we become human. This is what we're "here for."

And how does that happen? By being regularly immersed in the drama of God in Christ reconciling the world to himself, which is precisely the point of Christian worship—to invite us into that story over and over again, "character-izing" us as we rehearse the gospel drama over and over. If our loves are liturgically formed—if learning to love takes practice—then we need to be sure that the practices of Christian worship reflect the plot of the gospel, that the lineaments of Christian worship rehearse the story line of Scripture. Such an understanding of Christian worship is precisely what we find in the ancient heritage of the church. We don't need to reinvent the wheel, nor do we need to invent new liturgies. We can find gifts in what the Spirit has already given the church, inheriting and faithfully contextualizing the accrued wisdom of Christian worship.

We can sometimes be tempted to trade prayer for activism. But Hans Urs von Balthasar reminds us that worship is for mission.

> *Prayer*, both ecclesial and personal prayer, thus ranks higher than all action, not in the first place as a source of psychological energy ("refueling," as they say today), but as the act of worship and glorification that befits love, the act in which one makes the most fundamental attempt to answer with selflessness and thereby shows that one has understood the divine proclamation. It is as tragic as it is ridiculous to see Christians today giving up this fundamental priority—which is witnessed to by the entire Old and New Testament, by Jesus' life as much as by Paul's and John's theology—and seeking instead an immediate encounter with Christ in their neighbor, or even in purely worldly work and technological activity. Engaged in such work, they soon lose the capacity to see any distinction between worldly responsibility and Christian mission. Whoever does not come **to know the face of God in contemplation** will not recognize it in action, even when it reveals itself to him in the face of the oppressed and humiliated.[a]

a. Hans Urs von Balthasar, *Love Alone Is Credible*, trans. D. C. Schindler (San Francisco: Ignatius, 2004), 109.

Worship Restor(i)es Us

Formative Christian worship paints a picture of the beauty of the Lord—and a vision of the *shalom* he desires for creation—in a way that captures our imagination. If we act *toward* what we long for, and if we long for what has captured our imagination, then re-formative Christian worship needs to capture our imagination. That means Christian worship needs to meet us as *aesthetic* creatures who are moved more than we are convinced. Our imaginations are aesthetic organs. Our hearts are like stringed instruments that are plucked by story, poetry, metaphor, images. We tap our existential feet to the rhythm of imaginative drums. As we noted in chapter 1, Antoine de Saint-Exupéry captures this well: "If you want to build a ship, don't drum up people to collect wood and don't assign them tasks and work, but rather teach them to long for the endless immensity of the sea."

I thought about this again when I was in the Tate Britain museum in London and had the opportunity to see a painting that has always captivated me. Painted by one of the Pre-Raphaelites, Sir John Everett Millais (1829–96), the painting is called *The Boyhood of Raleigh*. Sir Walter Raleigh, you might recall, was one of Queen Elizabeth I's intrepid explorers. He established some of the first British colonies in what is now North Carolina. But he also twice set sail in search of the elusive El Dorado. In the painting, Millais imagines just what creates such an adventurer and explorer. His hypothesis? A good storyteller. Raleigh and a young friend sit entranced by a wizened old sailor who is pointing to an immense sea, captivating them with tales of what lies on the other side. The story, on Millais's interpretation, gives birth to a longing that will govern and direct all of Raleigh's life.

Stories capture our imagination and teach us to long for the endless immensity of God.

In a similar way, Christian worship should tell a story that makes us want to set sail for the immense sea that is the Triune God, birthing in us a longing for "a better country—a heavenly one" that is kingdom come (Heb. 11:16). The biblical vision of *shalom*—of a world where the Lamb is our light, where swords are beaten into ploughshares, where abundance is enjoyed by all, where people from every tribe and tongue and nation sing the same song of praise, where justice rolls down like waters and righteousness like an everlasting stream—is the vision that should be enacted in Christian worship. And that vision will *captivate* us, not just because we "know" it's what God wants, but because the tangible practices of Christian worship paint the picture, as it were—in the metaphors of the biblical story, the poetics of the Psalms, the meter of hymns and choruses, the tangible elements of bread and wine, the visions painted in stained glass—all of which works on our imaginations, teaching us to want.

Worship works as fiction does: both traffic in story and target the imagination. Thus an axiom for novelists is also relevant for worship leaders: show, don't tell. In a profound little book of literary criticism, *How Fiction Works*, critic James Wood delves into the very operation of literature. "Fiction does not ask us to *believe* things," he points out, "but to *imagine* them. 'Imagining the heat of the sun on your back is about as different an activity as can be from believing that it will be sunny. One experience is all but sensual, the other wholly abstract.'"⁹ Is there not a suggestive, analogical intuition here for Christian worship? "When we tell a story," Wood continues, "although we may hope to teach a lesson, our primary objective is to produce an imaginative experience."

Since the time of Aristotle, one of the tasks of literature has been described as *mimesis*, imitation. *Mimesis* is also a New Testament theme (see 1 Cor. 4:16; 11:1; Eph. 5:1; Phil. 3:17). But, Wood points out, this doesn't mean that literature and poetry are supposed to "copy" reality. It's actually about cultivating a sense of *plausibility*. The best art, Aristotle says, makes plausible what might otherwise seem impossible. It is a matter of *mimetic persuasion*: convincing us that this *could be.*

Isn't this what Christian worship is also meant to do, week after week? To let the Spirit of God, with whom nothing is impossible, convince us that *this could be*: that despite a million voices crying otherwise, the gracious good news of the gospel is *true*. It is one thing to understand the sentence "The dead shall be raised"; it is quite another to *feel* what it must be like if it is true that "he is risen!" But this is a conviction that happens on the register of the imagination.

Worship that restores our loves will be worship that restor(i)es our imagination. Historic Christian worship has a narrative arc that rehearses the story of redemption in the very form of worship—enacting the "true story of the whole world."[10] And it does so in a way that speaks in the language of the imagination, the part of us that understands *in* story. Intentional, historic liturgy restores our imagination because it sanctifies our perception—it implants the biblical story so deeply into our preconscious that the gospel becomes the "background" against and through which we perceive the world, even without "thinking" about it. Only when you are formed this deeply can you say as C. S. Lewis did, "I believe in Christianity as I believe that the sun has risen: not only because I see it, but because by it I see everything else."[11] This is a "belief" that you carry in your bones.

And the *way* worship does this is by inviting us, week after week, into a set of practices that don't just communicate information to our minds but conscript our loves and longings through disciplines that speak to our imagination, the deep aesthetic register on which we tacitly understand the world without ever putting it into words—at the level of our social imaginary. To be human is to inhabit some narrative enchantment of the world. Christian worship fuels our imaginations with a biblical picture of a world that, in the words of poet Gerard Manley Hopkins, is "charged with the grandeur of God."

Worship that restores us is worship that restories us. Worship that renews is worship that renarrates our identity at an unconscious level. In order to do that, Christian worship needs to be governed by the biblical story and to invite us in by speaking to our embodiment. It is this twofold conviction that informs historic Christian worship, which is why faithful retrieval of this heritage is a gift for the future of faith. Let's consider *how* the liturgical tradition embodies this.[12]

Plotlines: The Narrative Arc of Christian Worship

Across an array of traditions (hence its "catholicity," its universality),[13] historic Christian worship reflects a basic plot or narrative arc that centers on God's gracious reconciliation of all things to himself (Col. 1:20). Many have noted that historic

The fact that we are "character-ized" by stories is not lost on rival culture shapers. Consider, for example, the insight of media entrepreneur David Rose, who exhorts designers and entrepreneurs to "reenchant" the world through products:

> The final step of the Ladder of Enchantment is creating or adding to a story that will enchant the user. Why a story? We all think of our lives as stories, each with a main character (us), theme, and plot (interesting so far, but as yet unfinished). We also love to hear stories about others and even about things. **Stories hook into our curiosity**—what happens next?—and into our emotions: What would I do in that situation? Stories have the unique power to engage and, if they engage enough, to trigger empathy, enchant. Designers, having tapped the potential of personalizing, socializing, and gamifying, can work to embed a drama in our heads. They can involve us in a story so the narrative gains a purchase on both our minds and [our] hearts. It becomes part of our heritage, our folklore, our mythology. We can feel as if we are part of the action, even a central character in the tale.[a]

a. David Rose, *Enchanted Objects: Design, Human Desire, and the Internet of Things* (New York: Scribner, 2014), 203–4.

Christian worship invites a congregation into a story with four chapters:

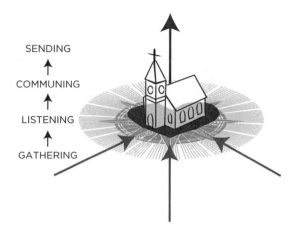

This narrative arc of Christian worship, passed down through the centuries, is a kind of macroreenactment of God's relationship to creation. Each moment is composed of further elements. For example, the opening "chapter"—**gathering**—unfolds with a *call* to worship, reminding us that God is the gracious initiator here, echoing our being called into existence by the Creator. In contrast to a worship service that vaguely begins when the music starts playing and parishioners slowly saunter in to join the crowd, a worship service that begins with the Call to Worship has already received a word from the God who is active in worship and who *wants* us there. (Notice how, already, this framing of Christian worship is countercultural, displacing the priority of self and our desire to have the world available to us on *our* terms.) So the Call to Worship is a weekly reenactment of the primacy and sovereignty of the Creator in our lives: just as we are called into being by the God who creates, so we are called into new life by that same God, who redeems us in Christ by the power of his Spirit. Just as God's creative power made us to be human, so the Spirit's renewing power will enable us to be human.

Having been called into God's holy presence and greeted by his grace, we become aware of his holiness and our sinfulness and thus are led into a time of confession[14]—a communal practice whereby we come face-to-face with our sins of both commission and omission, with our disordered desires and our complicity in unjust systems. To be called to confession week after week is to be reminded of a crucial chapter of the gospel story. What is lost when we remove this chapter from so many gatherings that purport to be Christian worship? We lose an important, *counter*-formative aspect of the gospel that pushes back on secular liturgies of self-confidence that, all week long, are implicitly teaching you to "believe in yourself"—false gospels of self-assertion that refuse grace. The practice of confession is a crucial discipline for reforming our loves.

But the Christian practice of confession is not a groveling mire of "worm theology," a kind of spiritual masochism, because there is never a moment of confession that isn't immediately met with the announcement of the good news of forgiveness and absolution. The good news of forgiveness is its own countercultural (and hence counter*formative*) practice that pushes back on the hopelessness and despair of a consumer gospel that can offer only goods and services, not true peace.

You can start to get a sense, I hope, of how historic Christian worship is organized around a plot that has a "narrative logic" to it. Having been graciously called into the presence of a holy but forgiving God, we now enter into the **listening** chapter of worship. This includes hearing the announcement of his law or will for our lives, which is not a burdensome yoke we try to "keep" in order to earn our salvation—we've already been reminded that we are forgiven in (and only because of) Christ. Rather, the law is now received as that gift whereby God graciously channels us into ways of life that are for our good, that lead to flourishing. The announcement of the law is how God invites us to live "with the grain of the universe."[15] We listen as we hear God's Word proclaimed, another opportunity for us to make the biblical story *our* story, to see ourselves as characters in the drama of redemption.

This culminates in our **communing** with God and with one another. We are invited to sit down for supper with the Creator of the universe, to dine with the King. But we are *all* invited to do so, which means we need to be reconciled to one another as well. Our communion with Christ spills over into communion as his body. There is a *social*, even *political*, reality enacted here: there are no box seats at this table, no reservations for VIPs, no filet mignon for those who can afford it while the rest eat crumbs from their table. The Lord's Table is a leveling reality in a world of increasing inequalities, an enacted vision of "a feast of rich food for all peoples, a banquet of aged wine" (Isa. 25:6). This strange feast is the civic rite of another city—the Heavenly City—which is why it includes our pledge of allegiance, the Creed. In this communion our hearts are drawn into the very heart of God's Triune life. Thus, in some ways the fulcrum of the liturgy is the *sursum corda*: "Lift up your hearts." In worship "we lift them up to the Lord." The Lord's Supper isn't just a way to remember something that was accomplished in the past; it is a feast that nourishes our hearts. Here is an existential meal that retrains our deepest, most human hungers.

Having been invited into the very life of the Triune God—having been re-created in Christ, counseled by his Word, and nourished by the bread of life—we are then sent into the world to tend and till God's good creation and to make disciples of every nation. The **sending** at the end of the worship service is a replay of the original commissioning of humanity as God's image bearers because in Christ—and in the practices of Christian worship—we can finally be the humans we were made to be. So we are sent out to inhabit the sanctuary of God's creation as living, breathing "images" of God. We bear his image *by* carrying out our mission to cultivate creation and invite others to find their humanity in this Story. Thus worship concludes with a benediction that is both a blessing and a charge to *go*, but to go *in* and *with* the presence of the Son, who will never leave us or forsake us—to go in peace to love and serve the Lord.

This is only the barest sketch of the "plotline" of historic Christian worship. In my suggestions for further reading at the end of the book, you'll find resources that will take you through this story line of worship in more detail. But in a sense, any book that summarizes the plot will never be the same as immersing yourself in the practices themselves. This is a cat you have to carry by the tail for yourself. The goal of any analysis or explanation can only be to help you appreciate what's at stake *in* the practices, to help you understand why we do what we do when we worship. Otherwise the rituals can seem to be merely "traditional"—or worse, superstitious, rote exercises. But once you see the biblical narrative that is embedded and carried *in* the practice, you should begin to see how and why worship is the heart of discipleship. Worship is the sacramental center of God's transforming grace. You might think of worship as the repair station for our erotic compasses. Or, as Calvin suggested, think of the church's worship as the gymnasium in which the Spirit puts us through the paces of a spiritual workout that restor(i)es our hearts. Some mornings you wake up, and let's be honest: you don't want to work out. Your bed is so comfortable and the world outside is so cold and it would be so easy to just stay where you are. But the people of God are not there, and the sacraments of the Spirit aren't there, and you know that even if you don't "feel" like it, you need the meal that is the Lord's Supper, you need the nourishment of the Word. You know the sort of person you want to be and know that immersing yourself in this Story is how the Spirit is going to change your habits.

Interlude: Some Tough Questions

Now, what if your congregation's worship doesn't look like this? What if you can't discern anything close to this narrative plot in the Sunday gatherings at your local church? Well, with some fear and trembling, let me say three things.

- First, look closely. This plotline isn't the sole property of "high church" liturgy. Don't miss the forest for the trees. Don't let a particular "style" distract you from noticing the narrative spine that runs through the worship service. However, if you find yourself in a congregation that constricts the word "worship" to one slice of the service—the music—then you're not likely to find the narrative arc we've just described. In which case:

- Try to be part of a solution. If you are a pastor or elder or worship leader, you have the opportunity to play a role in the renewal of worship in your congregation. If you are a parishioner, you can invite your leadership into a discussion that begins to consider the buried treasure of the church's liturgical tradition. In such endeavors toward renewal, frame the need in terms of the gifts for discipleship. Help your sisters and brothers see that we miss out on Spirit-empowered opportunities for counter- and re-formation when we leave the treasures of historic worship on the shelf, unpracticed. Don't frame this as a "recovery" project or a defense of "traditional" worship or a nostalgic return to some golden age. At stake in these historic Christian worship practices is the *future* of faith, not its past.

- Finally, if renewal doesn't seem possible, you might have to make a difficult decision, after much prayer and counsel, about worshiping elsewhere. I say this with the utmost caution and want to emphasize: the "perfect church" nowhere exists. But because I do believe that worship is the heart of discipleship—and hence that the church is at the heart of the Christian life—I also believe that for the sake of discipleship it is crucial to immerse oneself in a community of practice that exhibits the reformative potential we've been describing. Your heart is at stake.

Indeed, in many ways I think the future of orthodox, faithful, robust Christianity hinges on the renewal of worship. Charting a future for Christianity first requires some genealogical work: How did we get here? In this respect, Charles Taylor highlights a particular strand of modern Christianity that has had a significant impact on contemporary expressions, particularly evangelicalism. Taylor describes this as a dynamic of "excarnation."[16]

The term is deliberately provocative, running counter to a central tenet of our confession: the incarnation—the affirmation that God became human and took on flesh, that the eternal, immaterial God would condescend to become embodied, enfleshed, incarnate. This notion of incarnation is behind traditional Christian understandings of the sacraments—the conviction that material, embodied *stuff* mediates the eternal and divine. So in addition to the conviction that the human Jesus embodies God, Christians have also traditionally emphasized that creation itself is charged with the Spirit's presence.

But one of the unintended consequences of the Protestant Reformation, Taylor argues, was a disenchantment of the world. Critical of the ways such an enchanted, sacramental understanding of the world had lapsed into sheer superstition, the later Reformers emphasized the simple hearing of the Word, the message of the gospel, and the arid simplicity of Christian worship. The result was a process of *ex*carnation—of disembodying the Christian faith, turning it into a "heady" affair that could be boiled down to a message and grasped with the mind. To use a phrase that we considered above, this was Christianity reduced to something for brains-on-a-stick.

The "spirituality" of the spiritual-but-not-religious often imitates this sort of excarnate religion, sometimes without realizing it. The self-help spirituality of our wider culture is remarkably "Protestant," one might say. Give us a few inspirational aphorisms, some "thoughts for the day" to get us through the grind, a couple of poignant one-liners on the side of our Starbucks cups, and that's all the "message" we need to keep significance alive. This is spirituality cut to the measure of thinking things who inhabit a disenchanted cosmos.

Why does this matter for the future of Christianity? Because now that the whole world has been disenchanted and we have been encased in a flattened "nature," I expect it will be forms of reenchanted Christianity that will actually have a future. Protestant excarnation has basically ceded its business to others: if you are looking for a message, an inspirational idea, some top-up fuel for your intellectual receptacle—well, there are entire cultural industries happy to provide that. Why would you need the church? You can watch Ellen or Oprah or a TED talk.

But what might stop people short—what might truly haunt them—will be encounters with religious communities who have punched skylights in our brass heaven. It will be "ancient" Christian communities—drawing on the wells of historic, "incarnate" Christian worship with its smells and bells and all its Gothic peculiarity, embodying a spirituality that carries whiffs of transcendence—that will be strange and therefore all the more enticing. I make no claims that such communities will be large or popular mass movements. But they will grow precisely because their ancient incarnational practice is an answer to the diminishing returns of excarnate spirituality. In other words, historic Christian worship is not only the heart of discipleship; it might also be the heart of our evangelism.

Because when the thin gruel of do-it-yourself spirituality turns out to be isolating, lonely, and unable to endure crises, the spiritual-but-not-religious crowd might find itself surprisingly open to something entirely different. In ways that they never could have anticipated, some will begin to wonder if "renunciation" isn't the way to wholeness, if freedom might be found in the gift of constraint, and if the strange rituals of Christian worship are the answer to their most human aspirations. What Christian communities need to cultivate in our "secular age" is faithful patience, even receiving a secular age as a gift through which to renew and cultivate an *incarnational*, embodied, robustly orthodox Christianity that alone will look like a genuine alternative to "the spiritual."

The Gift of Confession

Let me highlight one example: the practice of confession and assurance of pardon. This is but one chapter in the narrative arc of Christian worship, but it might highlight what's at stake when we let elements of this story drop out of our worship.

In the 1980s, North American evangelicalism experienced an almost revolutionary innovation: what later came to be known as the megachurch. What defined this new dialect of evangelical Christianity wasn't really size but strategy. The philosophy of ministry and evangelism behind the megachurch movement was often described as "seeker sensitive." Sunday gatherings would be less focused on building up those who were already Christians and more focused on being hospitable to "seekers," those who were not yet Christians but were curious enough to consider attending an "event" that was accessible, welcoming, entertaining, and informative.

But in order for the church to be *that* sort of place it was going to have to feel less, well, *churchy*. If it was going to be sensitive to seekers, the church would have to remove those aspects of its practice and tradition that were alleged to be obstacles to the "unchurched." If the church was going to feel welcoming, it needed to feel familiar, accessible, and "cool," characterized by the sorts of professional experiences people associated with consumer transactions together with the thrilling enjoyment of a concert. The seeker-sensitive church would *feel* like the mall, the concert, and Starbucks all rolled into one—because those are places that people *like*, where they feel comfortable.

Not only would this change the architecture and decor of North American evangelical congregations; it would also significantly change the way we worship. "Traditional" liturgies were seen as dated, dusty, and—worst of all—boring. Other aspects of historic Christian worship, like the Lord's Supper, were thought to be just plain weird from the perspective of seekers. Instead, a seeker-sensitive congregation would have to de-emphasize certain aspects of Christian proclamation and worship in order to front-load those aspects of the gospel that feel more affirming. Less wrath, more happiness; less judgment, more encouragement; less confession, more forgiveness.

One common aspect of traditional Christian worship that was excised from seeker-sensitive congregations was the practice of corporate confession of sin. Historic worship always included a communal, public confession of our sin. Week in and week out, gathered before a holy God, the people of God would confess their failures and faults, their sins of omission and commission, saying they were sorry "for the things we have done and the things we have left undone." And that regular confession of our sins would always be answered by "absolution" and the assurance of pardon—the announcement of the good news that, in Christ, we are forgiven.

This regular, stark, uncomfortable confession of sin doesn't seem like something that would be "enjoyed" by seekers. It raises difficult questions and brings us face-to-face with disquieting truths about ourselves. It feels like the very opposite of being sensitive to those who are seeking.

But what if the opportunity to confess is *precisely* what we long for? What if an invitation to confess our sins is actually the answer to our seeking? What if we *want* to confess our sins and didn't even realize it until given the opportunity? In other words, what if confession is, unwittingly, the desire of every broken heart? In that case, extending an invitation to confession would be the most "sensitive" thing we could do, a gift to seeking souls.

Oddly enough, contemporary television seems to appreciate this truth. I can think of two stark examples that illustrate just this point.

The first is HBO's dark, disturbing, but stellar miniseries *True Detective*, in its first season starring Matthew McConaughey and Woody Harrelson as Louisiana detectives Rust Cohle and Marty Hart. The details of the narrative arc need not detain us here. I simply point to an episode in which Rust is seen as the go-to interrogator for the department. He is able to elicit confessions from almost anyone. His method, as he explains when asked how he does it, is rooted in a philosophy about human nature:

> Look—everybody knows there's something wrong with them. They just don't know what it is. Everybody wants confession, everybody wants some cathartic narrative for it. The guilty especially. And everybody's guilty.

Here is a truth the seeker-sensitive movement couldn't have imagined: people *want* to confess.

One can even find this in a BBC melodrama like *The Last Tango in Halifax*. Set in the charming environs of Yorkshire, the story intertwines two families, each with their own secrets and dark pasts. Late in season 2, a wayward daughter named Gillian makes a shocking, disturbing confession to Caroline, her new stepsister. The confession burbles up from some primordial need; indeed, it is veritably vomited out of Gillian—a point the director makes a little more obvious by then showing us Gillian vomiting into the sink. Not at all subtle, the image gets at the visceral, bodily impulsion to confess. When Caroline, still in shock, asks Gillian why she told her, Gillian can only say that she *needed* to do so, even *wanted* to do so.

This desire to confess may seem counterintuitive. Obviously the seeker-sensitive movement assumed this was the *last* thing non-Christians wanted to do. Why in the world would sinners want to be confronted with their sin? But I wonder if these artifacts of popular culture actually suggest that the opposite is true: deep down, we already know what's true about our faults and brokenness. If that's the case, rituals that invite us to confess our sins are actually gifts. The rites of confession have their own evangelistic power.

This is poignantly captured in the last lines of Graham Greene's novel *The Quiet American*. After implicating himself in fatal dealings involving a young man named Pyle, the narrator, Fowler, issues an apology:

> "I'm sorry, Phuong."
>
> "What are you sorry for? It is a wonderful telegram. My sister—"
>
> "Yes, go and tell your sister. Kiss me first." Her excited mouth skated over my face, and she was gone.
>
> I thought of the first day and Pyle sitting beside me at the Continental, with his eye on the soda fountain across the way. Everything had gone right with me since he had died, but how I wished there existed someone to whom I could say that I was sorry.

The good news, of course, is that there is.

The Poetics of Confession

I have emphasized that Christian worship rehabituates our loves because it embeds us in—and embeds in us—a different orienting Story, the story of God in Christ reconciling the world to himself. But Christian worship doesn't just rehearse the outlines of this story in a kind of CliffsNotes, bullet-pointed distillation of some "facts." It does so in a way that is storied, imaginative, and works on us more like a novel than a newspaper article. Story isn't just the *what* of Christian worship; it is also the *how*.

If the biblical narrative of God's redemption were just information we needed to know, the Lord could have simply given us a book and a whole lot of homework. But since the ascension of Christ, the people of God have been called to gather as a body around the Word and the Lord's Table, to pray and sing, to confess and give thanks, to lift up our hearts so they can be taken up and re-formed by the formative grace of God that is carried in the rites of Christian worship. Something is going on in the worship of the gathered/called congregation beyond simply the dissemination of information.

The same thing that is going on in worship today was going on in the ancient worship of the people of God—all the way back to Israel—which has also been characterized by a certain *poetics*. If God meets us as liturgical animals who are creatures of habit, he also meets us as imaginative animals who are moved and affected by the aesthetic. This key intuition about formation is as old as the Psalms.[17] Desire-shaping worship isn't simply didactic; it is poetic. It paints a picture, spins metaphors, tells a story.

In this way the gospel isn't just information stored in the intellect; it is a way of seeing the world that is the very wallpaper of our imagination. Stories that sink into our bones are the stories that reach us at the level of the imagination. Our imaginations are captured poetically, not didactically. We're hooked by stories, not bullet points. The lilt and cadence of poetry have the ability to seep down into the fine-grained regions of our imagination in a way that a dissertation never could. The drama and characters of a novel stick with us long after the argument of a book has been forgotten—and then change how we move in the world. Anyone who has truly *absorbed* Dante or Dickens or David Foster Wallace inhabits the whole world differently. Stories stick.

Actually, the writer David Foster Wallace describes something like what I'm trying to describe here, but in a very different context. In a stunning essay on the "liquid grace" of tennis icon Roger Federer, trying to describe the regimens of formation that could create the prowess of a Federer, Wallace names what I'm fumbling to describe:

> Successfully returning a hard-served tennis ball requires what's sometimes called "the kinesthetic sense," meaning the ability to control the body and its artificial extensions through complex and very quick systems of tasks. English has a whole cloud of terms for various parts of this ability: feel, touch, form, proprioception, coordination, hand-eye

coordination, kinesthesia, grace, control, reflexes, and so on. For prom-
ising junior players, refining the kinesthetic sense is the main goal of
the extreme daily practice regimens we often hear about. The training
here is both muscular and neurological. Hitting thousands of strokes,
day after day, develops the ability to do by "feel" what cannot be done
by regular conscious thought.[18]

"To do by 'feel' what cannot be done by regular conscious thought":
that's not a bad description of the goal of discipleship. To conform to the image of the Son is to have so absorbed the gospel as
a "kinesthetic sense," a know-how you now carry in your bones,
that you do by "feel" what cannot be done by conscious thought.
You have been remade in Christ such that there are ways you love
him that you don't even know. You have a Christlike "feel" for
the world, and you act accordingly "without thinking about it."

This kind of "sense" is deeper than knowledge; it's a know-
how you absorb poetically, on the register of the imagination.
Formative worship speaks to us—shows us,[19] touches us, shapes
us—on this level. Let me return to the example of confession to
try to illustrate the point. The practice and communal discipline
of confession is an important aspect of the Story that should govern our being-in-the-world. But if the sensibility that confession
should generate is going to be carried in our bones, then even our
confession needs to be more poetic than didactic. In other words,
how we confess makes a difference as to whether this practice will
truly be formative.

Consider two very different examples of prayers of confession.
The first is a contemporary prayer whose provenance I'll leave
unidentified, for reasons that should be clear in a moment:

> Today we confess that we have not done enough to protect our planet.
> We confess that we have failed to insist that our government set stan-
> dards based on precaution. We confess that we, as consumers, have
> allowed companies to release dangerous toxins that destroy fragile
> ecosystems and harm human beings, especially those among us who
> are most vulnerable.

> God of justice, help us understand the need and send a clear signal
> to our political leaders about making the crucial choice between the
> present path of "destructiveness"—or the morally responsible path
> of compassion and respect for life, acknowledging our dependence
> upon you and our interconnectedness with all creation.

Not much danger of this being described as "poetic." It is driven
by a pure fixation on content, aims to be primarily didactic, and
would be very difficult for a congregation to recite together precisely because it has no rhythm or cadence that makes it sing. For
this reason it will also be a confession that is quickly forgotten.

Contrast this with a historic prayer of confession that might
sound familiar precisely because its poetry has made it so enduring.

> Most merciful God,
> we confess that we have sinned against you
> in thought, word, and deed,
> by what we have done,
> and by what we have left undone.
> We have not loved you with our whole heart;
> we have not loved our neighbors as ourselves.
> We are truly sorry and we humbly repent.
> For the sake of your Son Jesus Christ,
> have mercy on us and forgive us;
> that we may delight in your will,
> and walk in your ways,
> to the glory of your Name. Amen.

You can feel the lilt and rhythm of this, even if it's the first time
you've ever read or heard it. Its use of parallel and parataxis, sym-
metry and series, allusion and alliteration all make it "work" on
us below the radar of consciousness.

Now imagine hearing this on the lips of a congregation, over
and over again, where it takes on life like a song. The point of a
poetic confession is not to make it pretty: we are owning up to
our sin and faults and failures, after all. But it is the poetry of this
confession that makes it stick and enables it to seep down into the

deep wells of our imagination—which means it is also latent there, ready to rise to our lips throughout the week, giving us confidence in the promise that if we confess our sins he is faithful and just to forgive (1 John 1:9). Thus the prayer is not just a "rite" for a Sunday morning; it is a gift that goes with us throughout our week as we seek to follow Christ.

And then give thanks in your heart because you never, ever, *ever* hear this prayer without immediately hearing the good news:

> Almighty God have mercy on you,
> forgive you all your sins
> through our Lord Jesus Christ,
> strengthen you in all goodness,
> and by the power of the Holy Spirit
> keep you in eternal life. Amen.

And you move through your day inhabiting a different Story, with the humility of confession ready on your lips, hungry for the mercy of God, longing to embody it for your neighbor.

5

GUARD YOUR HEART

The Liturgies of Home

"We love because he first loved us" (1 John 4:19). This truth is the nourishing conviction of what I've been describing: the model of human beings as lovers and the vision for discipleship that grows out of it. The divine initiative of love for us—even while we were enemies (Rom. 5:8–10)—is the first grace that both makes possible and provokes our love. And note that John's remarkable, beautiful claim is not just that we love *God* because he first loved us, but that we *love* because he first loved us. Even our disordered loves bear a backhanded witness to the fact that we are made in God's image.

Swiss theologian Hans Urs von Balthasar captures this in an image that is both beautiful and biblical, a metaphor that is natural and supernatural at the same time. "After a mother has smiled at her child for many days and weeks," he notes, "she finally receives her child's smile in response. She has awakened love in the heart of her child, and as the child awakens to love, it also awakens to knowledge."[1] It's like we love in order to know. But we are loved into loving. Noting the priority of the mother's initiative, Balthasar continues: "Knowledge . . . comes into play, because the play of love had already begun beforehand, initiated by the mother, the transcendent." There is a natural but iconic picture here of a reality that is transcendent and eternal:

> God interprets himself to man as love in the same way: he radiates love, which kindles the light of love in the heart of man, and it is precisely this light that allows man to perceive this, the absolute Love: "For it is the God who said, 'Let light shine out of the darkness,' who has [shone] in our heart to give the light of the knowledge of the glory of God in the face of Christ" (2 Cor. 4:6). In this face, the primal foundation of being smiles at us as a mother and as a father. Insofar as we are his creatures, the seed of love lies dormant within us as the image of God (*imago*). But just as no child can be awakened to love without being loved, so too no human heart can come to an understanding of God without the free gift of his grace—in the image of his Son.[2]

The smile of the cherishing mother that evokes the smile of the infant is a microcosm of a cosmic truth: that God's gracious initiative in the incarnation—"he first loved us"—is the provoking smile of a Creator who meets us in the flesh, granting even the grace that allows us to love him in return. The picture is powerful because it is so tangible and embodied: you can picture the chubby cheeks, smell that one-of-a-kind new baby scent, hear the tch-tch-tch soundtrack of a suckling child, and then watch the serene smile of wonder and love that washes over a mother's face. That smile, Balthasar suggests, is its own kind of sacrament—a means of grace, a conduit of love. The Creator of the universe meets us in the same way, enfolding us into his care by meeting us in the Son become flesh.[3] Jesus is the smile of God. That incarnational impulse to provoke our responses is continued in his body in the tangible ways he nurses and nourishes our faith, giving us bread, wine, and water along the way.

But the metaphor is suggestive in another way: it is a reminder of the ways that love is incubated in the home, that the household is also a deeply formative (or *de*formative) space that teaches us how to love from infancy. We love because he first loved us, but we learn *how* to love at home.[4] This is part of an important reality that needs to be realized and named. Obviously an hour and a half on Sunday morning is not sufficient to rehabitate hearts that are daily immersed in rival liturgies. Yes, gathered, congregational worship is the heart of discipleship, but this doesn't mean that communal worship is the *entirety* of discipleship. While communal worship calibrates the heart in necessary, fundamental ways, we need to take the opportunity to cultivate kingdom-oriented liturgies throughout the week. The capital-*L* Liturgy of Sunday morning should generate lowercase-*l* liturgies that govern our existence throughout the rest of the week. Our discipleship practices from Monday through Saturday shouldn't simply focus on Bible knowledge acquisition—we aren't, after all, liturgical animals on Sunday and thinking things for the rest of the week. Rather, our day-to-day practices need to extend and amplify the formative power of our weekly worship practices by weaving them into our everyday liturgies.

There are all kinds of other spaces where we can and should be intentional about the liturgies that govern our rhythms, and we should see this as an opportunity to extend the formative practices of worship into other sectors of our life. Recognizing worship as the heart of discipleship doesn't mean sequestering discipleship to Sunday; it means expanding worship to become a way of life.

So if we need to be intentional about the liturgies of Christian worship in the congregation, we should be equally intentional about the liturgies of the household.[5] More specifically, we should be attentive to the rhythms and rituals that constitute the background hum of our families and should consider the *telos* toward which these activities are oriented. The frenetic pace of our lives means we often end up falling into routines without much reflection. We do what we think "good parents" do. And we might think these are just "things that we do" without recognizing that they may also be doing something *to* us. This chapter is an invitation to take a kind of liturgical audit of our households, recognizing their power to calibrate our hearts and acknowledging that our domestic rituals might need to be recalibrated as a result of our auditing work.

However, we should also consider how the liturgies of the household *grow out of* and *draw us into* the liturgies of the congregation. No home or family can be its own "church"; no household is a substitute for the household of God (Eph. 2:19). We all need to locate our households in the household of God and to situate our families within the "first family" of the church.[6] To do this, we first need to see the ways that the church's worship teaches us *how* to be families and households. Then we need to consider how our household (lowercase-*l*) liturgies can be nourished by and can propel us back into the (capital-*L*) Liturgy of the body of Christ.

Liturgical Lessons for Home-Makers

I have argued that in worship we learn on levels we don't always realize. The practices of Christian worship carry biblical truths that are sometimes more caught than taught; they picture what God desires for us in ways that might be more powerful than explanations. Embedded in the church's worship are important pictures of what flourishing homes and families look like. Making those implicit pictures more explicit can provide wisdom for how we might then liturgically order our home. Let's consider just two powerful pictures of the household in worship: baptism and marriage.

First, we need to relinquish our tendency to think of baptism "expressively." Baptism isn't primarily a way for us to show our faith and devotion. As with worship more generally, God is the agent here. Baptism is a sacrament precisely because it is a means of grace, a way that God's gracious initiative marks and seals us. It is the sign that God is a covenant-keeping Lord who fulfills his promises even when we don't. This is why, since the time of the early church, households have been baptized (Acts 16:33; 1 Cor. 1:16), and it is why, historically in "catholic" Christianity, believing parents present their children for baptism.[7] As a sacrament, baptism is not a bottom-up expression of *our* faith but a top-down symbol of God's gracious promises. He chose us before we could believe; he loves before we even know how.

Baptism signals our initiation into a *people*. Through baptism God constitutes a peculiar people who make up a new *polis*, a new religio-political reality (what Peter Leithart calls a "baptismal city"[8]) that is marked by the obliteration of social class and aristocracies of blood. It is a motley crew: "not many of you are wise by human standards, not many were powerful, not many were of noble birth" (1 Cor. 1:26 NRSV). But that is the mark of the city of God, God's upside-down kingdom: "God chose what is foolish in the world to shame the wise; God chose what is weak in the world to shame the strong; God chose what is low and despised in the world, things that are not, to reduce to nothing things that are" (1 Cor. 1:27–28 NRSV). The citizens of the baptismal city are not just "have-nots"; they're "are-nots"! And yet they are chosen and commissioned as God's image bearers, God's princesses and princes who are empowered to be witnesses of a coming kingdom and charged with the renewal of the world.

So baptism both makes and signifies a social reality, which is why it is situated in the context of gathered worship. While perhaps only one person is being baptized, all of us participate in this sacrament. We, the congregation, are not there merely as spectators. On a minimal level, the ritual should call to mind our own baptism, thus rehearsing for us our own "pledge of allegiance," reminding us that we are citizens of another city. This is also why some churches have water at their entry, providing a tangible occasion for recalling *whose* we are. As we enter for prayer or worship, the stirring, touching, and perhaps self-anointing with water is a visceral reminder that we are a marked people. Baptism is a practice that reconstitutes our relation to other social bodies such as the family and the state.

So what does baptism signal about families? What understanding of family is carried in this worship practice? What are we learning on a gut level when we participate in this rite? The baptismal liturgy calls for us, the congregation, to also make a covenantal promise. For instance, when children are presented for baptism, the minister turns to the congregation and asks something like,

> Do you, the people of the Lord, promise to receive these children in love, pray for them, help instruct them in the faith, and encourage and sustain them in the fellowship of believers?[9]

The congregation then responds, "We do, God helping us." The covenant binds us together as a community, a "city" (a *polis*, as the Greeks would say—a "republic" of sorts). If we are a new configuration of the *polis*, we are also a new configuration of the family, "the household of God" (Eph. 2:19 NRSV). In the household of God there is a relativizing of bloodlines. Our promises in baptism—as parents and as a congregation—signal that what counts as "family" is not just the closed, nuclear unit that is so often idolized as "the family." Thus, if Christian congregations are truly going to live *out of* and *into* the significance of baptism, they will need to become communities in which the bloodlines of kin are trumped by the blood of Christ—where "natural" families don't fold into themselves in self-regard.[10] Orthodox theologian Alexander Schmemann puts this quite pointedly: "A marriage which does not constantly crucify its own selfishness and self-sufficiency, which does not 'die to itself' that it may point beyond itself, is not a Christian marriage. The real sin of marriage today is not adultery or lack of 'adjustment' or 'mental cruelty.' It is the idolization of the family itself, the refusal to understand marriage as directed toward the Kingdom of God."[11]

Instead, the church constitutes our "first family,"[12] which is both a challenge and a blessing. On the one hand, it challenges yet another sphere of rabid autonomy in late modernity: the privacy of the family. On the other hand, it comes as a welcome relief: we don't have to raise these kids on our own!

The "idolization" of the family noted by Schmemann results in an almost impossible pressure on the family to function as a closed, self-sufficient, autonomous unit. As Schmemann laments, "It is not the lack of respect for the family . . . [but] the idolization of the family that breaks the modern family so easily, making divorce its almost natural shadow. It is the identification of marriage with happiness and the refusal to accept the cross in it."[13] The rituals of political liberalism (whether one is ideologically more "liberal" or more "conservative") paint a picture of the family as the incubator of good citizens, dutiful producers, and eager consumers at the same time that it shuts up the family in a private, closed home as part of the American ideal of independence.[14] The result is an unbearable weight placed on the family. "The predominant theology of the family" that is implicit in liberalism, McCarthy remarks, "isolates it with the formidable and lonely task of being a whole communion." But baptismal promises counter such a configuration: love and its obligations traverse the boundaries of "private residences" and "nuclear families" because they initiate us into a household that is bigger than that which is under the roof of our house. The promises in baptism indicate a very different theology of the family, which recognizes that "families work well when we do not expect them to give us all we need." Instead, the social role of the family that is configured by baptism is to be a family "dependent upon a larger social body. . . . In theological terms, family is called to be part of the social adventure we call the church."[15]

Thus baptism becomes an almost subversive sacrament that revolutionizes many of the notions of social life that we have inherited, even those that claim to be "conservative" and "religious." For as McCarthy elsewhere notes, "Baptism establishes a communion that qualifies our relationships of birth."[16] Just as baptism relativizes the bloodlines of the priesthood, so it situates and positions even the bloodlines of the home and family. Our baptismal promises attest to the fact that "the church is our first family." And "if the church is our first family, then our second homes should be defined by it, and our doors ought to be open to the stranger, the sick, and the poor."[17] Baptism opens the home, liberating it from the burden of impossible self-sufficiency, while also opening it to the "disruptive friendships" that are the mark of the kingdom of God.[18]

For this reason, one of the most important decisions we can make regarding faith formation in our homes is the congregation to which we commit ourselves. Wise faith formation begins in the hub of the church's gathered worship life. So one of the best decisions parents can make for their children's faith journey is to immerse them in a congregation whose liturgical practices enact the Story we've described above. (We'll discuss this more in chapter 6.)

A tacit understanding of the family and household is enacted in baptism; it is also in our wedding ceremonies. We learn *how* to be families in these rituals, even if we're not consciously thinking about it. When you attend your cousin's wedding, and then your roommate's wedding, and then your nephew's wedding, you are absorbing "under the radar" a vision of what a family should look like—like learning to carry a cat by the tail. So this too is a slice of our cultural immersion where we need to cultivate our critical, "apocalyptic" capacities to read with discernment the cultural liturgies of weddings.

We might be tempted to think of the explosion of the wedding industry as good news, as a sign that our culture is beginning to value marriage and family—until we read between the lines and actually discern the vision of the good life that is carried in our cultural patterns.

Try to look with new eyes at a familiar phenomenon. Look at the "wedding season" through the liturgical lens. What do you see?

'Tis the season to make weekend forays to events that will light up Facebook and swamp Instagram with a deluge of sepia-toned photographs. Years of hopes pinned on Pinterest will become a reality as we dance long into the night. It's not Lollapalooza or Bonnaroo: it's your cousin's wedding.

The excitement has been building ever since that first Facebook post—the one with the video of him proposing to her against the industrial-chic backdrop of the Brooklyn Navy Yard while a band whose members have beards and lots of banjos "surprised" them with a serenade. The video went viral, of course, so the bar was raised for the wedding itself. The invitations arrived encased in 1950s cigar tins and featured overlapping images of their tattoos on handmade paper, complete with vintage postage stamps for the RSVPs. The wedding reception will be catered by Korean taco food trucks, and the band from the engagement is going to play an encore, only with more mandolins, under candlelit canopies draped with hops as everyone enjoys the groom's craft beer. The wedding has its own tumblr and, of course, its own hashtag. And everyone goes home with their own mouth organ inscribed with the bride's and groom's names. No one will forget this day, mostly because it will be scrupulously photographed, posted, shared, tweeted, and uploaded. And we all know: the internet never forgets.

The wedding industry generates an estimated 49 to 51 *billion* dollars annually. Wedding shows like *Say Yes to the Dress* and *Bridezillas* constitute their own category of "reality" TV. My completely unscientific assessment of Pinterest suggests that wedding-related aspirations make up about 80 percent of the content of the internet. Gone are the days when, as elderly saints in my congregation tell me, couples were married on Sunday night at church. A wedding today is too important to waste: it hasn't happened until the wedding video, à la Wes Anderson, is posted on Vimeo. "We're getting married! We've got a *wedding* to plan!"

Doesn't all of this prove that our society values marriage more than ever?

Not so much. In fact, estimates indicate that the revenues of the divorce industry mirror those of the wedding industry (a reality that has even spawned its own documentary).[19] Our interest is in the spectacle of the wedding—the event in which we get to be center stage, display our love, and invite others into our romance in a way they'll never forget. The wedding industry thrives on competition, novelty, and one-upmanship (and we haven't even yet considered the impact of the Facebook feeds on those who are single). As Charles Taylor might put it, in our "age of authenticity," weddings are caught up in the dynamics of "mutual display": what's important is *being seen*. It's why we spend more time fixated on the spectacular flash of the wedding event than on the long slog of sustaining a marriage.

But the implicit mythology of Wedding Inc. also reflects how we approach marriage. Indeed, the myths we load into weddings almost doom marriages to fail. Weddings are centered on the romantic "coupling" of two star-crossed lovers, as if marriage were an extended exercise of staring deep into one another's eyes—with benefits. But even then, a spouse is one who *sees* me, will meet my needs, will fulfill my wants, will "complete me." Even our romantic coupling becomes a form of self-love (hilariously captured in *Saturday Night Live*'s "MeHarmony" spoof).

This romantic picture is already enacted in the honeymoon: to kindle your marriage, you need to "get away," retreat from the drudgery of the workaday world (which is, apparently, matrimonial poison). For your marriage to last, according to this logic, you'll have to keep planning "date nights" and romantic escapes for just the two of you, to "keep the fire alive." And by all means, don't have children too soon: they are, according to this myth, the equivalent of a marital buzzkill, because marriage is romance, and romance is just the two of you.

Too many weddings are spectacles in which we celebrate *your* dyadic bliss. We're there more as spectators than as partners. And in that sense, these weddings are often preludes to the sorts of

Ben Birchall / ©PA

The rituals of the wedding "industry" are liturgies of narcissism, as illustrated in this Banksy image.

marriages that follow. When lovers are staring into one another's eyes, their backs are to the world—a self-involved inwardness stingingly captured in the Banksy "Mobile Lovers" image above.

This "romantic," just-the-two-of-us view of love and marriage suffuses almost all of our cultural narratives and is enacted in many of our wedding rituals—especially those that imagine themselves as primarily "expressive." Indeed, it is so woven into the warp and woof of our social imaginary that we can't imagine an alternative (perhaps not even in the church, which is equally susceptible to buying into this mythology). Isn't a wedding the realization of our romantic dreams? And isn't marriage the idyll of a sort of perpetual wedding/honeymoon?

Contrast the vision of family carried in these cultural liturgies—and played out in television dramas and romantic comedies—with the countercultural, biblical vision that is carried in an Orthodox wedding rite.[20] The rite has two "movements" or stages. The first is the Service of Betrothal. In the entrance or vestibule of the church, the priest asks both the groom and the bride a question. To the

Our friends Christopher and Jennifer Kaczor tell a powerful story about family that starts before they were married. Chris recalls the situation in a short essay, **"The Myth of Vampire Children"**: "My university experience, like that of so many others, was rich. I was a college athlete and editor of a campus paper. I had discovered a love for philosophy, and was thinking about going to graduate school. Life was great, an ocean of potential. And then I got the phone call that changed everything. Only one sentence of the conversation really mattered: 'I'm pregnant.'"[a]

At that moment, he thought his world was coming to an end. "I had bought into the myth that children are nothing more than a drain," he recounts: "a financial drain, an emotional drain, a dream-killing drain. I viewed children as little more than vampires, sucking the lifeblood out of their parents"—exactly the myth fostered by the "romantic" view of marriage.

But that all changed when Elizabeth finally arrived. Over the course of raising her, along with six other children, Chris realized that children were a gift to their marriage, not an interruption or threat. They are invitations to "put on" virtues like gratitude, humility, patience, and steadfastness. All those years ago, he confesses, "I thought that having a baby was the worst thing that could have happened to me. I could not have been more wrong." Children are like the wooden cross to the myth of vampire children: "Having a child isn't an 'end' to the good things of life," Chris concludes; "it is an 'and' to the good things of life."

a. Christopher Kaczor, "The Myth of Vampire Children," *First Things*, February 2015, 17–18.

groom: "Have you, Nicholas, a good, free, and unconstrained will and a firm intention to take unto yourself to wife this woman, Elizabeth, whom you see before you?" And to the bride: "Have you, Elizabeth, a good, free, and unconstrained will and a firm intention to take unto yourself to husband this man, Nicholas, whom you see before you?" Each in turn replies, "I have," and these are the *only* words they will speak in the ceremony. This won't be an expressive opportunity for them to "show their love." There's no fixation on novelty in the idiosyncratic writing of their own vows.

The actor and agent here is the Lord, the church's Bridegroom, and their lives as husband and wife (and as mother- and father-to-be) are here being taken up into that life. The Triune God is the center of this ceremony, exhibiting a vision of marriage in which this is also true. This is beautifully signaled in vows that echo their baptism "in the name of the Father, and of the Son, and of the Holy Spirit."

With rings placed on their fingers as part of the Service of Betrothal, the groom and bride are then led in procession from the narthex into the sanctuary—a performative way of showing that their marriage is to be brought into the kingdom of God. Their family is embedded in the first family that is the body of Christ. "By taking the 'natural' marriage into 'the great mystery of Christ and the Church' [Eph. 5]," Schmemann comments, "the sacrament of matrimony gives marriage a *new meaning*; it transforms, in fact, not only marriage as such but all human love."[21] When the "natural" institution of their marriage is ushered into the sanctuary, it is "the entrance of marriage into the Church, which is the entrance of the world into the 'world to come.'"[22] This is a picture of our natural desires for the supernatural finding their *telos* in Christ. It is a foretaste of kingdom come.

This brings us to the second movement or stage of the rite: the Service of Crowning, where the couple's own story is embedded within the sweeping Story of salvation history, of God's faithfulness to his Bride, the people of God. The prayers during this movement of the service celebrate biblical exemplars—husbands and wives, mothers and fathers, including those who struggled with hope and barrenness. The bride and groom are being narratively surrounded with a cloud of witnesses to what faithful families look like—families that, not surprisingly, look a lot different than the families on *Bridezillas*. This stage culminates in the couple's crowning, in which they are literally crowned as servant and handmaid of God "in the name of the Father, and of the Son, and of the Holy Spirit." This illustrates, as Schmemann puts it, that "each family is indeed a kingdom, a little church, and therefore a sacrament of and a way to the Kingdom."[23] Their marriage is a mission; together they will *bear witness*. Schmemann captures this beautifully:

> This is what the marriage crowns express: that here is the beginning of a small kingdom which *can* be something like the true Kingdom. The chance will be lost, perhaps even in one night; but at this moment it is still an open possibility. Yet even when it has been lost, and lost again a thousand times, still if two people stay together, they are in a real sense king and queen to each other. And after forty odd years, Adam can still turn and see Eve standing beside him, in a unity with himself which in some small way at least proclaims the love of God's Kingdom. In movies and magazines the "icon" of marriage is always a youthful couple. But once, in the light and warmth of an autumn afternoon, this writer saw on the bench of a public square, in a poor Parisian suburb, an old and poor couple. They were sitting hand in hand, in silence, enjoying the pale light, the last warmth of the season. In silence: all words had been said, all passion exhausted, all storms at peace. The whole life was behind—yet all of it was now *present*, in this silence, in this light, in this warmth, in this silent unity of hands. Present—and ready for eternity, ripe for joy. This to me remains the vision of marriage, of its heavenly beauty.[24]

These are not crowns of royal privilege: they are the crowns of the martyrs, bearing witness to Christ. Husband and wife are crowned as witnesses, called to sacrifice. This is why the sacrament of Holy Matrimony ends with the Eucharist, at the Lord's Table, where *all* who are present are nourished by the body and blood of the Crucified One. And henceforth *every* Lord's Supper will be another wedding feast, another way we learn how to be married, in which we see and smell and taste the story of the Groom who laid down his life for his Bride. Every Sunday is a marriage-renewal ceremony.

You're not going to learn *that* in the liturgies of *The Bachelorette* or in the customized expressivist weddings that revolve around the couple. To the contrary, we need to become aware of how much we have "learned" about marriage and family from these cultural liturgies and intentionally seek to roll back their influence by immersing ourselves in counterliturgies found in the body of Christ. Embedding our own households and families in the household of God at once decenters our tribe, with its tendency to become an idol, and simultaneously centers us in the only community that can sustain us: the Triune God.

Our households—our "little kingdoms"—need to be nourished by constant recentering in the body of Christ. Week after week we bring our little kingdoms into the kingdom of God. Communal, congregational worship locates the family in the sweep of God's story and in the wider web of the people of God.[25] From there we are sent back into our households and families, where we then

---

The marriage liturgy signals that marriage is a call to serve others; a husband and wife make a covenant with God and one another so that they can become a tiny "people" who are sent, like Israel and the church, to bear witness to the nations. Marriage is for the common good. This is beautifully expressed in the conclusion to the United Methodist service of Christian marriage, which culminates in a "Sending Forth."

The pastor turns to the newlywed couple with both a blessing and a charge:

> God the Eternal keep you in love with each other,
>> so that the peace of Christ may abide in your home.
> Go to serve God and your neighbor in all that you do.

Then the pastor turns to the congregation with a similar charge and blessing:

> Bear witness to the love of God in this world,
>> so that those to whom love is a stranger
>> will find in you generous friends.
> The grace of the Lord Jesus Christ,
>> and the love of God,
>> and the communion of the Holy Spirit
>> be with you all.
> Amen.

have an opportunity to extend the church's worship into our "little churches." So let's think about the liturgies that can frame the places where we eat our daily bread—for in important ways, the formative power of Christian worship is amplified when our daily lives echo and expand those rhythms.

Guard Your Hearts

The image of the nuclear family has always been an ambiguous one for me. Of course it's meant to convey a picture of a *centered* family, anchored by a mom and a dad, with children orbiting around them as satellites, together serving as one of the basic units of society—an "atomic unit," if you will. (Part of the sad state of our age is that such a picture is now taken to be quaint and antiquated.) But having been raised during the denouement of the Cold War and shaped by movies like *Red Dawn,* for me the notion of a "nuclear" family also carried connotations of a bomb shelter or concrete bunker, a fortress to protect us from the threats of a menacing world.

The metaphor is stark but not entirely off base. Granted, there are extreme versions of this that are insular and fearful (versions held by those we might call the "doomsday preppers" of Christian parenting). But we rightly have a sense of caution when it comes to the influence of the world on our families, especially on our children. Indeed, it's a biblical admonition: we are both incubators and defenders of our children's hearts and minds, stewards of their imaginations, responsible for their instruction. And thus it is only natural that we should be their defenders, on guard like sentinels watching in the distance for oncoming threats. When the father of Proverbs 4 admonishes his son, saying, "guard your heart" (v. 23), the father's instruction is itself part of that defense.

But what if we're missing the real threats? What if we're constructing defenses against the intellectual blasts of ideas and messages from the world but not insulating against the sort of toxic radiation that can seep through our intellectual defenses?

This happens when we parent our children as if they are thinking things. Every parenting strategy, like every pedagogy, assumes something about the nature of human beings (insofar as children are human beings—and trust me, I remember the days when that was hard to believe). Having drunk from the Cartesian wells of modernity, we tend to treat our children as intellectual receptacles, veritable brains-on-a-stick, and we parent and protect them accordingly. We try to foster their faith by providing them with biblical knowledge, catechizing them to give us the right answers, and then gradually equipping them to also discern the false teachings the world will throw at them. If we humans are basically thinking things, then both our defenses and our instruction should be primarily didactic and theological.

But what does it look like to parent *lovers*? What does it look like to curate a household as a formative space to direct our desires? How can a home be a place to (re)calibrate our hearts?

That changes things. It means we should be concerned about the ethos of our households—the unspoken "vibe" carried in our daily rituals. Every household has a "hum," and that hum has a tune that is attuned to some end, some *telos*. We need to tune our homes, and thus our hearts, to sing his grace. That tuning requires intentionality with regard to the hum, the constant background noise generated by our routines and rhythms. That background noise is a kind of imaginative wallpaper that influences how we imagine the world, and it can either be a melody that reinforces God's desires for his creation or it can (often unintentionally) be a background tune that is dissonant with the Lord's song. You could have Bible "inputs" every day and yet still have a household whose frantic rhythms are humming along with the consumerist myth of production and consumption. You might have Bible verses on the wall in every room of the house and yet the unspoken rituals reinforce self-centeredness rather than sacrifice.

Thus each household and family does well to take an audit of its daily routines, looking at them through a liturgical lens. What Story is carried in those rhythms? What vision of the good life is carried in those practices? What sorts of people are made by immersion in these cultural liturgies?

Such household liturgical audits will be highly contextual. A household of college students will have an entirely different set of routines than will a young couple with infants and toddlers in the house—and each of them will be enticed by and invited into different types of cultural liturgies. A multigenerational household in Los Angeles will have a very different set of routines—and hence temptations—than will a retired couple in Winnipeg. The powerful cultural liturgies of youth sports have almost no bearing on college students who live together, and the litanies of a "club" culture don't impinge on the life of that couple with young children. Our liturgical temptations and deformations are always contextual. Each of us should assess the routines our household takes for granted, precisely because those are the routines we don't usually think about—and hence, whose formative power we don't recognize. We think of them as "things we do" and might not recognize that they're doing something to us.

Having critically assessed the routines we're caught up in, we can then attend more intentionally to recalibrating countermeasures. First and foremost, our households need to be caught up in the wider household of God: the liturgies of our homes should grow out of, and amplify, the formative liturgy of Word and Table.[26] As Michael Horton so winsomely says in his book on worship, *A Better Way*, biblical worship draws us into the drama of Christ-centered redemption.[27] That liturgical formation "character-izes" us: it weaves us into the story of God in Christ and thus shapes our character. The formative liturgies of a Christian home depend on the ecclesial capital of the church's worship.

What would it look like to let the rhythms of gathered Christian worship set the tune for our daily household tempo?

Family worship will be formative to the extent that it taps into our imagination, not just our intellect. To do so, such worship needs to traffic in the aesthetic currency of the imagination—story, poetry, music, symbols, and images. Such worship will be tactile, tangible, incarnate. (Think of all the prophet Jeremiah's object lessons as a biblical model here.) Children are ritual animals who absorb the gospel in practices that speak to their imaginations.

This is an important reason to make music an aspect of family worship. As Augustine is often paraphrased as having said, "He who sings prays twice." There is something at work in the lilt of a melody and the poetry of a hymn that makes the biblical story seep into us indelibly.

This is also a reason to invite your family into the rhythms of the liturgical calendar or the "Christian year."[28] The rhythms of Advent and Christmas, Epiphany and Pentecost, Lent and Easter are a unique way to live into the life of Jesus. The colors of these seasons can become part of the spiritual wallpaper of your home, shaping the ethos of a family. The royal purples of the King, the bright white of Christmastide, and the fire red of Pentecost all create a kind of symbolic universe that invites us into a different story.

These seasons also come with their own tactile rituals. Families can enjoy creating an Advent wreath together each year, and then children can tangibly participate in lighting the candles of hope, love, joy, and peace—sometimes known as the Prophet's candle, the Bethlehem candle, the Shepherd's candle, and the Love candle—looking forward to lighting the Christ candle on Christmas. During Lent, families can observe a form of fasting together in which the growling of hungry bellies is a visceral way to learn about hungering and thirsting after righteousness. There is a physicality to such household worship that encourages us to understand the gospel anew, in ways that endure in our imagination and thus shape how we make our way in the world.

This is an important point: the formative rituals of the household are not just "private" exercises; they have a *public* impact

precisely insofar as household formation, like communal formation and worship, ends in *sending*. We are not creating a "pure"
household into which we withdraw and retreat in order to protect
ourselves from the big, bad world. That would be to shirk our mission to "go." Instead, we want to be *intentional* about the formative
rhythms of the household so that it is another recalibrating space
that forms us and prepares us to be launched into the world to
carry out both the cultural mandate and the Great Commission,
to bear God's image to and for our neighbors.

We might say that the sacramental power of Christian worship
"enchants" our everyday lives, reminding us that the world we inhabit is not a flattened "nature" but rather a creation charged with
the presence and power of the living Spirit. The world into which
we are sent is a world that calls for our culture-making, inviting
our mercy and compassion. Creation is always more than we see.
What might appear "natural" is suffused with God's grandeur. It
is in worship that we learn to inhabit the world in this way, as an
environment charged by the presence and activity of God. We can,
therefore, look for ways to let the world's enchantment spill over
into the so-called mundane spaces of our lives. We can look for
ways to cultivate "enchanted households" that reflect this reality.

Consider just a couple of examples. My friend Rev. Chris
Schutte, pastor of Christ Church Anglican in Phoenix, told me
that in their congregation each person who is baptized receives a
baptismal candle to take home. They are encouraged to bring out
the candle each year and to light it on their baptismal anniversary.
The sight and scent of the tiny flame comes "loaded," you might
say, with the memory of what the Spirit has done—and is doing.
The candle also serves to remind them that the candles of their
"natural" birthday are taken up and sanctified by their baptismal identity in Christ: this is their "new creation" birthday. The
lighting of the candle is a tangible reminder of *who* they are and
whose they are, and weaving this rite into their home reinforces
that their baptism is *for* the world.

A congregation we have been part of also provided a tangible take-home reminder of baptism. At the baptism of a child, the child and her family receive a small clay ornament made by a local artist in the congregation. Inscribed on one side of the ornament are the words "I am your God," and on the other side, framed by a rainbow, are the words "You are my child." The rainbow is a symbolic reminder that God keeps his covenant, keeps his promises to his people. This simple ornament is, in a sense, "enchanted" by the context in which it is given: it's almost as if the sacramental power of baptism washes over onto this ornament. Many parents then hang the ornament in the child's room for the years to come—over their baby's crib, near their child's bed, above their teenager's desk. The ornament hangs there faithfully during good times and bad, when the child ardently follows and errantly strays, its steady presence a physical reminder of the God who is faithful even when we are faithless (2 Tim. 2:13). In this way, a simple physical gift becomes an enchanted object that keeps teaching us to hope.

Building Cathedrals at Home

In *Communities of Practice*, educational theorist Etienne Wenger recounts the story of two stonecutters. Each is asked what they're doing. One responds, "I am cutting this stone in a perfectly square shape." The other responds, "I am building a cathedral."[29]

I can imagine the first stonecutter pausing at the second's reply and then saying to himself, "That's right. I forgot. We *are* building a cathedral."

When I hear this story it reminds me of the *Building Cathedrals* blog, which brings together the wisdom of seven Catholic women, all graduates of Princeton University, who are, as they put it, "seeking to build our families just as the architects of the great cathedrals built their detailed masterpieces: day by day, stone by stone, with attention to details that only He will see." There are a lot of tedious aspects to stonecutting and masonry, and yet all are crucial to the grand project of cathedral building. So too with parenting: little things matter. Micro rituals can have macro implications.

For example: never underestimate the formative power of the family supper table. This vanishing liturgy is a powerful site of formation. Most of the time it will be hard to keep the cathedral in view, especially when dinner is the primary occasion for sibling bickering. Yet even then, members of your little tribe are learning to love their neighbor. And your children are learning something about the faithful promises of a covenant-keeping Lord in the simple routine of that daily promise of dinner together.

Then there will be nights when the mundane subsides and all the accumulated capital of those meals together gives you the opportunity to invite your children to see the world anew. Don't underestimate the significance of a dinner-table education. This hit home for me again recently. Around the Smith family table one night, our conversation veered toward a heartbreaking story of a twelve-year-old boy who had marched to a playground and killed a nine-year-old neighbor with a knife. He then knocked on a nearby door, asked to call the police, confessed his crime, and told the officer he wanted to die.

As my wife, Deanna, recounted this story at dinner, our youngest son's blood began to boil with anger, an adolescent expression of sadness for the boy who was killed. *What could possibly drive a young boy to do this?* But Deanna wasn't finished with the story, and *how* she told the rest was a lesson in moral discernment and compassion.

How, indeed, could a boy do that to another? As we already suspected, the horrors of the young man's abuse and neglect emerged. Sadly, it almost became understandable why this boy wanted to die. Though not an excuse, it was clear that this murderer was a victim too. Tears began to well up in Deanna's eyes as she tried to get our son to imagine the unimaginable. She filled in the picture:

the filth of the boy's so-called home, its tables covered with drug paraphernalia but its cupboards bare. The boy's body was riddled with bruises and scars from abuse, and he arrived at school hungry almost every morning. Deanna patiently, yet tearfully, tried to get Jack to realize that almost everything he took for granted in his own life was absent from this young man's world. Jack sat silently as he absorbed all of this. Not even a sixteen-year-old boy could suppress his tears by this point.

That night, one of our older boys just happened to be home from college and had joined us for dinner. He was quiet through all of this, seemingly aloof, and gathered his plate without a word and went into the kitchen. But then, in the mirror on the dining room buffet, I could see him behind me, hunched over the counter, sobbing quietly, learning to lament. Even mourning takes practice: resisting the distractions that insulate us from facing up to the tragedy of the world in which we find ourselves, we need to teach our children to mourn for neighbors who bear the brunt of injustice, even though we grieve as those with hope (1 Thess. 4:13). Sometimes in this fallen world the best thing we can do is teach our children how to be sad.

When we situate our households in the wider household of God and extend the liturgies of worship to shape the ethos of our homes, we resituate even the mundane. When we frame our workaday lives by the worship of Christ, then even the quotidian is charged with eternal significance. Our "thin" practices take on thicker significance when nested in a wider web of kingdom-oriented liturgies.

In our dining room hang several vintage posters from the "victory gardens" movement during World War II, when those on the home front planted gardens in order to help alleviate pressure on a rationed food supply. The gardens that were planted in parks and church yards also became catalysts for community, helping neighbors cultivate friendship around a common task and the natural sacrament of getting your hands dirty.

These posters represent everything that my wife, Deanna, is passionate about: creation and community, food and friendship. My favorite is one that brings together our passions: "Cultivate Imagination," it exhorts. Amen.

You could say that the posters are the wallpaper of a way of life that Deanna has fostered in our household—rhythms centered on garden and kitchen, the common labor of tilling the soil and the common life fostered by the collaboration of cooking. When I look at our household through a liturgical lens, I see deeply formative "liturgies" that Deanna has invited all of us into. She invites us into seasonal rhythms of the garden's life, which is like creation's liturgical year. In February we start thinking about seeds and look longingly for springlike Easter hope. In the spring we learn patience as the ground thaws and the soil emerges and we wait for the earth to warm to the reception of seeds and plants. In summer we submit ourselves to the discipline of attention—to a garden that requires constant care—while also enjoying the unique delights of emergence when shoots and leaves and blossoms begin to appear. The community at Hillcrest Garden is a beehive of activity each day and night, and we meet a cross section of our city that reminds us who our neighbors are. Even while we contend with recalcitrant weeds, we begin to enjoy the harvest and the new color that each day brings—in tiny tomatoes and squash blossoms and the splendor of zinnias. All of this demands a kind of Sabbath slowdown in the midst of our otherwise "efficient" and "productive" lives.[30] To grow a garden is to inhabit a different economics.

I'll never tire of Deanna's squeals of glee as she finds new abundance each day: a zucchini that seems to have emerged overnight; an eggplant that is just beginning its vegetal life; a cherry tomato vine laden with fruit. In Deanna's daily walk around the garden, in a mode of grateful reception, she models virtues for our children: a hopeful expectancy, a grateful diligence, and a tangible gratitude.

These garden liturgies find their end in the kitchen as we eat the fruit of our labor. Here, too, I've watched Deanna foster an

The formative power of household rituals.

entire ethos that has enfolded our children into a vision of the good life. They have been apprenticed through rituals that reinforce the importance of community, friendship, and hospitality. While they learn how to slice onions, or why we only eat "happy" cows, the kids are being inducted into a Story about what flourishing looks like—a vision of flourishing that is bigger than their individual happiness, even bigger than their individual souls. These liturgies don't focus on Bible reading, yet they teach us to attend to God's creation. These rituals might not include formal prayer, and yet they are a kind of tactile expression of hope. And their formative significance lives off of the wider web of liturgies in which they are nested. The significance of these household liturgies is oriented by the Liturgy of the body of Christ. The table at home is an echo of the Lord's Table; the communion of the saints is given microcosmic expression in the simple discipline of daily dinner together. There is an ongoing dance between the rhythms of gathered worship and the rhythms of our "sent" lives Monday through Saturday.

6

TEACH YOUR
CHILDREN WELL

Learning by Heart

I grew up in Embro, a small village in southwestern Ontario. Embro was so small we didn't even have the one stoplight needed to make it into the ranks of one-stoplight towns. Like many who grew up over time in a particular environment, I knew Embro like the back of my hand—I knew it by heart, you might say. But the *way* I knew Embro is suggestive for how we think about teaching and learning "by heart."

Imagine you were driving through Embro in 1984 and for some reason had occasion to stop. Imagine seeing me in the parking lot by the Highland Restaurant, trying to master a freestyle BMX maneuver. You catch my attention and say, "Excuse me, son. Could you tell me where St. Andrew's Street is?" Despite the fact that I'm thirteen and have lived in Embro my whole life, chances are I'm not going to be able to help you. Why? Because the *way* I know Embro is not the kind of knowledge that you find on a map. I learned this town on the ground, from the bottom up. I learned Embro as someone who lived *in* it, not by looking *at* it or reflecting *on* it. Learning street names is an abstract sort of knowledge—a maplike knowledge that sees a town from a vantage point ten thousand feet in the air. Map knowledge is the knowledge of a spectator, not an inhabitant; it is how an outsider sees the village, not a native. I know this town differently because I learned it differently.

So I might not be able to answer your question about the location of St. Andrew's Street, but I can get to the baseball diamond or the hockey arena with my eyes closed. I know where Shawn's house is, and where the post office is, and how to get to Christine's place, and the shortcut to Vinegar Hill. I know where to find the best jumps for my bike and a back way into that spooky old mansion up by the United Church. I might not be able to answer your question, but I know this town by *feel*. I know my way around because the knowledge I have is what David Foster Wallace called "kinesthetic": it's know-how that I carry in my bones. It's a knowledge that I caught, that I learned by doing. I didn't even realize I was learning.

What would it look like to "learn" the Christian faith the way I learned my way around Embro? What would it mean to have a "feel" for God's creation the way I had a feel for my hometown? What if learning to have the "mind of Christ" was less like memorizing a map and more like learning how to live and move and have our being in Christ? How can we form and educate young people so that they know the gospel in their bones? What if we could absorb a biblical understanding of the world like we were natives of God's good creation?

What if education weren't first and foremost about what we *know* but about what we *love*?

This raises questions about how we approach education and the formation of young people in the Christian faith in a variety of contexts—in schools and youth groups, in Sunday school and catechism, in campus ministries and college classrooms. Formation is an inherently educational project (indeed, the French word for "training" is *formation*); but this also means that education is an inherently formational project, not just an informational endeavor. As Stanley Hauerwas puts it, "All education, whether acknowledged or not, is moral formation."[1] We need to think carefully about the *telos* of Christian education as well as the pedagogies by which we induct young people into the faith.[2] In this chapter, I want to invite you into several different spaces where young people are educated in the faith—from church nurseries to middle school classrooms to college residence halls.[3] If we appreciate that human beings are liturgical animals, we will see young people with new eyes—as the ritual creatures they are, hungry for rites that give them rhythms and rhymes they can live into.

God Desires True Worshipers

When you walk into the primary Sunday school area at St. George's Episcopal Church in Nashville, you'll immediately notice that this space echoes the sanctuary upstairs. The usual flannelgraphs and Bible memory verse posters are conspicuously absent; in their place is something that feels like a worship laboratory of sorts. Like the hands-on experience in science instruction, where you get to light the Bunsen burner and concoct chemical reactions that fizz and pop, this space for young disciples offers children the chance to be immersed in the same kinds of realities they experience upstairs in the sanctuary. Here children learn the faith in ways that are more tactile than didactic. This is where they learn to carry a cat by the tail, as it were.

At a first station is a visual representation of the church's liturgical calendar that invites the children to locate where we are in the year that takes us through the life of Christ. Alongside the colorful image of the church year is a wooden version of the calendar, with a dial and markers that invite a kind of godly play—a way that children learn without even realizing they are being taught.

And yet, in this tangible instruction that invites them into the wider body of Christ—indeed, invites them to worship with the communion of the saints across the centuries—these children are already "catching" the Story of God's gracious reconciliation of all things. Even time is redeemed in Christ.

In a culture that is fixated on novelty and the thrill of the new, everything seems to be in flux and up for grabs. What fascinates us today will be "so five minutes ago" tomorrow. In a world where the only constant is a steady stream of changing images, it can feel like the ground beneath us is shifting sand.

Unfortunately, Christianity can sometimes fall prey to the same tyranny of the contemporary. In the name of "relevance," we keep "updating" the faith to appear au courant. The result, however, is the same groundlessness. In such versions of the faith, "church history" amounts to the life story of the church planter who started our congregation. The treasures and riches of our "catholic" Christian heritage—the millennia of the Spirit's faithful leading through history—are neglected and ignored. Instead, we try to reinvent the wheels of faith, and they are often a bit "wonky."

This is precisely why inducting Christians—especially young people—into the **heritage and legacy of catholic Christianity** can be a gift in a postmodern age. Like Elisha's army getting a glimpse of the angels that surrounded them (2 Kings 6:16–17), young people introduced to the historic disciplines of the church will also meet a communion of saints who surround them.

This is powerfully portrayed in the Cathedral of Our Lady of the Angels in Los Angeles. Rather than the typical stained-glass "hall of saints" surrounding the worshiping congregation, the cathedral is home to a series of tapestries by artist John Nava. The tapestries portray the exemplary lives of saints such as Boniface and Bridget of Sweden, Aquinas and Katharine Drexel. But interspersed with these historic figures in the church are the faces of boys and girls from contemporary Los Angeles. They are not only surrounded by this communion of the saints; they are also part of this ongoing story.

Beside the liturgical calendar station is another station devoted to baptism. Here, each week, children are reminded of their own baptism in tangible ways that draw out its significance: a white baptismal gown can be touched and asked about; water is there to wet their fingers, stirring sanctified memories of promises God made to them in the sacrament; the catechist invites them into this story again and again while giving them "something to do with their hands," so to speak. Through their godly play, the gospel sinks in.

In the corner is a space that invites the children to "play church," but with guidance into its significance and meaning. In durable wood you'll see tiny reproductions of sacred sites from the sanctuary: a pulpit with the Bible upon it; a baptismal font with the cross emblazoned on it; a candle and a cross like the one children see processed at the beginning of worship; a banner that signals the color of the current liturgical season. At another station are the mundane yet magical elements they see at Communion. These child-sized versions of the church's elements of worship are themselves imbued with an incarnational pedagogy: meeting children *where they are* in ways that answer their piqued curiosities, letting them handle and touch and ask about the rhythms of the people of God into which they are being enfolded.

Overlooking the entire learning space is an image of a third-century statue of the Good Shepherd from the catacomb of Domitilla, which also connects the children to ancient Christians through the inheritance of art. This image evokes the powerful metaphor of Jesus as the Good Shepherd in a way that meets the eye and speaks to the heart. On the shoulder of the shepherd is a vulnerable lamb, and every one of the little lambs in this space is reminded of the Good Shepherd who will carry them when they stray. It is just the sort of image and metaphor that gets lodged in your unconscious as a child, an imaged truth you then carry with you for the rest of your life—into your teens and eventually into your twenties, when you might drift from the faith, neglect these practices, and wander off into trouble, making a hundred bad decisions and winding up in some corner of the city and some way of life you could never have imagined when you were seven. Now that you're here, you're partly angry and partly embarrassed, so you have avoided the church like the plague. You're sick and tired of all the self-righteousness of religious people, not to mention the fact that you've acquired a slew of intellectual doubts about this whole "Christianity" thing, and it's easy enough to convince yourself that you're above it all. But what catches you short on some lonely evening of despair isn't a doctrine that you remember or all those verses you memorized from the book of Romans. What creeps up on you is the inexplicable emergence of this image of the shepherd from the deep recesses of your imagination's storehouse. With the image comes the story of a shepherd who is willing to leave the ninety-nine goody-two-shoes sheep who've done everything right in order to find that one stubborn, recalcitrant lamb. This image has stirred neurons in your stomach, it feels like, and somehow now you're in the middle of that story as that shepherd goes looking for the one wayward lamb, searching steadfastly. When he finds the bleating lamb cowering in a crevice, you can see the shepherd gently cradle the sheep and lift it out of its predicament with a smile and an encouraging, "C'mon, little guy." Then he hoists you on his shoulders, and you can't wait to be carried home.

That is an understanding of the gospel that is implanted not through merely didactic information transfer. It is an understanding of the gospel that is a kind of know-how, a knowledge you carry in your bones. And it is the sort of seeped-in conviction that is fostered by the kind of learning space I've just described. This space for learning the faith—being formed *in* the faith—is the fruit of what is known as "The Catechesis of the Good Shepherd," a model of children's ministry that draws on the wisdom of Maria Montessori's vision of engaged, embodied pedagogy.[4] The learning all takes place in an environment called "the atrium," a sacred space curated by teachers who are conscious of being "catechists," an ancient discipline that helps those new to the faith understand why we do what we do when we worship. This is *liturgical* catechesis. Instead of instruction in the faith that is centered on an abstract framework of doctrine lifted from the outline of systematic theology, liturgical catechesis is an induction into the faith that begins from what Christians *do* when we gather to pray around Word and Table. It is learning that is rooted in prayer. It is discipleship that bubbles up from worship. It is a pedagogy that is rooted in the conviction that we pray before we know, we worship before we "worldview." The worshipers the Father desires (John 4:23) are formed, not just *in*formed. That formation should begin with children's ministry that grabs hold of the imagination.

Youth Ministry for Liturgical Animals

Contrast the atrium of Good Shepherd catechesis with a very different scene. You walk into a kind of loft space that combines various elements of an arcade, a coffee shop, a dance club, and a family rec room. The room is dripping with energy, an unrelenting sense of scripted happiness that is synonymous with being "upbeat"—even while trying to communicate that this is a place where young people can "chill." Above all, it is trying very hard to be a place where young people *want* to be. Some kids are gathered around an Xbox playing video games, much as they would in a friend's basement. Others are lounging on couches, looking at Instagram and vaguely chatting with one another, catching up on their week. Still others are sticking close to tables laden with donuts and juice and M&Ms.

Eventually these little tribes are gathered together as one clan so that the program can begin. They are here instead of in gathered worship in the sanctuary (more likely in this context to be referred to as an "auditorium" than as a "sanctuary"). This program is their substitute "service." The liturgy will look familiar to them: A raucous band takes center stage, a routine widely familiar from concerts and music clubs. The band leads the group through a rousing set of triumphant praise songs and then into a quiet set of introspective, heartfelt, eyes-closed, hands-raised meditations. Whatever spell has been cast, however, is largely broken by an abrupt change of gears when a comedy troupe comes onstage to lighten the mood and let everyone know that following Jesus can be *fun*. The cheery atmosphere then creates room for a hip young teacher to emerge with either a broadly moralistic message ("don't drink, don't smoke, and above all, don't have sex") or a generically therapeutic message ("we're just here to love on you," as if the gospel were one big hug)—always communicated with the primary concern of not sounding *boring*. The best stories in this message come from film clips and pop music lyrics, reinforcing a sense that Christianity is "relevant" but at the same time subtly communicating a certain irrelevance of the Bible. Having been fed a vaguely biblical message, though in a more palatable package—kind of like choking down medicine hidden inside a piece of candy—the young people are dismissed with promises of more fun next weekend.

You wouldn't know it, but the entire "program" we've just witnessed is designed by *fear*—not *for* fear; *by* fear. It is the creation of a generation of parents and adults who are terrified that their children—the proverbial next generation—will leave the church and leave the faith. And they've convinced themselves that the primary reason young people will wander away from Christ is because they are bored. It's as if these adults overheard the nineties grunge band Nirvana shrieking, "Here we are now: entertain us!" but completely misunderstood the point. The result has been an approach to youth ministry that has reflected two disastrous decisions.

First, we have stratified the one body of Christ into generational segments, moving children and young people out of the ecclesial center of worship into effectively "parachurch" spaces, even if they're still officially in the church building. By doing so, we have tacitly denied the unity and catholicity of the body, worshiping in ways that run counter to Paul's remarkable proclamation that "there is one body and one Spirit, just as you were called to the one hope that belongs to your call; one Lord, one faith, one baptism; one God and Father of all, who is over all and through all and in all" (Eph. 4:4–6). More significantly, given our concerns about formation and the rehabituation of our loves, this segmentation of the body of Christ into generational castes eliminates one of the most powerful modes of habit-formation: imitation. If young people are always and only gathered with and by themselves, how will they learn from exemplars, those model saints in the local congregation who have lived a lifetime with Jesus?

Second, we have turned youth ministry into an almost entirely expressivist affair, surmising that what will "keep" young people in the church is a series of opportunities for them to sincerely exhibit their faith. Instead of embodied worship that is formative, we have settled for a dichotomy: an emotive experience as a prelude to the dispensation of information, thirty minutes of stirring music followed by a thirty-minute "message." While you might not immediately guess it, such dominant paradigms in youth ministry are actually held captive to thinking-thingism: the anti-intellectual fixation on entertainment is really just a lack of confidence in formation. While we might assume that the emotionalism of contemporary youth ministry is anti-intellectual, in fact it is tethered to a deeply intellectualist paradigm of discipleship: the whole point of keeping young people happy and stirred and emotionally engaged is so that we can still have an opportunity to deposit a "message" into their intellectual receptacles.

But we need to face a sobering reality: keeping young people entertained in our church buildings is not at all synonymous with forming them as dynamic members of the body of Christ. What passes as youth ministry is often not serious modes of Christian formation but instead pragmatic, last-ditch efforts to keep young people as card-carrying members of our evangelical club. We have confused keeping young people in the building with keeping them "in Christ."

In many cases we have already ceded their formation to secular liturgies precisely by importing those liturgies into the church under the banner of perceived relevance. So while young people might be present in our youth ministry events, in fact what they are participating in is something that is surreptitiously indexed to rival visions of the good life. The very form of the entertainment practices that are central to these events reinforces a deep narcissism and egoism that are the antithesis of learning to deny yourself and pick up the cross (Mark 8:34–36). While we might have many young people who are eager participants in all the entertaining events we stage for them, such participation is not actually forming their hearts and aiming their desires toward God and his kingdom as long as the default liturgies of such events are built on consumerist rituals and the rites of self-concern. Indeed, in our eagerness to keep young people entertained, we might only be swelling the ranks of those who cry, "Lord, Lord, didn't we attend every lock-in and campout and beach volleyball event in your name?" (cf. Matt. 7:21–23). In other words, we shouldn't be fooled by those who stick around merely to be entertained. Effective Christian formation of young people might *look* like failure for a time.

While contemporary youth ministry encourages hands-raised, heartfelt sincerity, in fact such paradigms reflect the "excarnation" of Christian faith in modernity (Charles Taylor's term, discussed above in chapter 4). Having reduced Christianity to a message, we create an emotional experience as a gateway to dispensing the message. But this is a sign that we have given up on *in*carnate modes of formation bequeathed to us in liturgy and the spiritual disciplines. Instead, we have created youth ministry that confuses extroversion with faithfulness. We have effectively communicated to young people that sincerely following Jesus is synonymous with being "fired up" for Jesus, with being *excited* for Jesus, as if discipleship were synonymous with fostering an exuberant, perky, cheerful, hurray-for-Jesus disposition like what we might find in the glee club or at a pep rally. The result, I would caution, can be disastrous. If we effectively communicate to young people that being a serious follower of Jesus is synonymous with being an extrovert for Jesus, then all of our young people who simply are not wired that way are going to quietly assume they can't be Christians. If the exuberance of the energetic youth pastor is taken to be exemplary, then all sorts of young people will mistakenly conclude that they simply can't be Christians. And so the unintended consequence: in the name of curating an exciting, entertaining "experience" to keep young people in the faith, we end up only creating consumers of a Jesus message while disenchanting vast swaths of other young people who simply can't imagine signing up for a Jesus glee club.

For those young people who are either scared or suspicious of happy-clappy versions of youth group Christianity, ancient Christian disciplines and historic Christian worship can be received as a life-giving gift. When you have only seen forms of piety that value spontaneous expression and clichéd sincerity, to be given the cadences and rhythms of the Book of Common Prayer can be like receiving the gift of tongues. In my experience, many young people are intensely ritual animals without realizing it. And when they are introduced to habit-forming practices of Christian faith, invited into ways of following Jesus that are ancient and tested, their faith is given a second life. They receive the disciplines not as burdensome duties but as gifts that channel their devotion and shape their faith. Instead of relying on their own internal piety and willpower (which is a wrong-headed way to think about discipleship anyway), young people experience historic practices of prayer and devotion as gifts of grace in themselves, a way that the Spirit meets them where they are. To receive the Psalms as the prayer book of the church is to have found a buried treasure right in the middle of the Bible.[5] Regimens of devotion like the Divine Office or *The Divine Hours* provide grooves for their faith to gear into, a tangible, historic way to align their desires with the grain of the universe.[6] The emphasis is no longer on their performance or expression; instead, such practices cultivate a posture of grateful reception of the Spirit's action.

Receiving these historic practices of worship and discipleship also connects young Christians to a faith that is ancient, thereby connecting them to a *body* that is older than their youth pastor and wider than their youth group. This is not insignificant for a life of authentic Christian faith. To follow Christ—to be *in Christ*—is to be enfolded in his body, which is a deeply social reality. This pushes back against the rites of autonomy and independence that are replete in late modern culture and that reduce us to privatized individuals with only tangential relationships to others. Such notions of autonomy and independence have seeped into the church, creating privatized versions of Christianity that prize a "personal relationship with Jesus" but can make little sense of why we need to be enfolded into his body. In contrast, the ancient disciplines of the church are gifts we share, inherited from the communion of saints. In historic practices we learn how to be a *community* of faith, not just a collection of atomistic individuals who happen to love the same Savior.

There is also a sense in which these strange historic rites of the church catholic serve to reenchant the world for those immersed in our secular, disenchanted age. One of the problems with contemporary youth group spirituality is that it seems to operate according to the same principles as any other "event": a kind of manipulated, managed "experience" that essentially relies on natural strategies, pulling the same heartstrings with the same lever as any other concert or football game or pep rally. The very similarity we wanted in order to keep young people entertained is precisely what makes them suspicious that there's nothing really *transcendent* going on here. Thus our well-intentioned Christian events end up naturalizing the world and leading to disenchantment. In contrast, the strange rites of ancient Christian worship carry in their very "weirdness" a disorienting haunting of transcendence. Young people aren't going to meet the ascended Lord of history in an event that feels like every other production they've ever attended. Indeed, while they might never articulate it, their departure from such versions of Christianity likely grows out of a suspicion that Christianity is nothing more than a production, like every other production. In contrast, the odd simplicity and charged weirdness of historic Christian practices are enchanted in ways that can't be explained and can thus be the stage for an encounter with the transcendent Lord in ways that help us imagine God anew.

I've witnessed this firsthand as a college professor who has watched a generation of young evangelicals wrestle through their disenchantment with the Christian faith only to find their way back again by remembering things the ancient church already knew. I've seen the jaded cynicism bred into twenty-year-olds by the manufactured spirituality of youth ministry and "Christian camp" culture, walked with students through their anger and frustration and bitterness, and watched them find new life when they discover the historic practices of the faith. Having been exhausted by the frenetic exuberance of expressivist worship, young Christians find room to breathe in the silence and simplicity of Taizé contemplation. If their youth group experiences knocked the wind out of them, the Book of Common Prayer gives them a way to breathe again. Having seen through the slick productions of the churches of their youth—where the band *performing* onstage is shrouded in smoke and lights—these young people find their faith again in the "smells and bells" of Christian worship whose pedigree is ancient.

I've also seen the power of this as a father. If raising four kids has taught us anything, it's this: children love tradition. In our house, to do anything even twice is to risk the kids' owning it as a "tradition." Indeed, we still enjoy "second-day-of-school cake" because one time, years ago, Deanna baked a cake on the second day of school and the kids immediately seized upon it. (We also

The contemplative, historic worship of the Taizé community in France draws young people from around the world.

now enjoy "third-day-of-school ice cream," and I've been angling for "fourth-day-of-school deep-dish pizza.") Kids want to be part of something bigger and older than they are, something that has a kind of ancient stability and endurance about it that testifies to God's faithfulness. But if children are traditional animals, they are also ritual animals. And the sad fact is that our youth ministries have treated them as thinking things that need to be entertained when, in fact, what they really crave is not liberation from ritual but rather liberating rituals. Have we failed to realize that while we're trying to entertain them, our young people are waiting for us to *form* them?

This brings to mind one of my most cherished memories as a father. During my first sabbatical, which we spent in Cambridge, England, we were given the opportunity to spend a few days in Paris thanks to free accommodations provided by a friend. We took a ferry from the white cliffs of Dover, disembarked in Calais, then drove our English car with its right-side steering wheel on the right side of French roads all the way down to Paris. Over the next few days, we looked for ways to explore the City of Light on our meager budget. That basically meant a lot of walking and seeing the *outside* of things. One day we traced a walk through the streets of Montmartre that led us through the neighborhood inhabited by the Impressionists and pictured in the movie *Moulin Rouge*. As we prepared to wend our way through the city for a few hours, we gave each of the kids a two-euro coin. "You can spend this any way you like," we told them (without breaking it to them that this wasn't likely to buy very much).

While in Montmartre, we made our way into Sacré-Coeur Basilica, which overlooks the red roofs of Paris. The space is, to say the least, enchanted. But my memory of the interior of the basilica pales in comparison to another memory I cherish. Our oldest child was (and still is) precisely the sort of young person who was not wired for extroverted piety and the exuberance of youth group spirituality. If one mistakenly identifies sincere Christian faith with that kind of expressivism, one will worry that those who don't "display" their faith don't *have* faith. But I was disabused of this confusion that day in Paris when I saw my oldest son, whose faith was quiet and understated, use his only two euros to light a candle in Sacré-Coeur. Here was a way for him to pray that was tangible and visceral—like the Spirit gave him a handle to grab hold of. The light of that candle was an epiphany.

Youth ministry seems to always be in search of the next big thing. But what if we should be looking *behind* us? The formation of young people in the faith requires us to give up our fixation on expressivist piety and to embrace the heritage of ancient disciplines and practices that carry the faith in ways that are tangible and tactile and—yes, admittedly—strange. Such strangeness is what makes them habit-forming, knocking off the edges of our narcissism and pushing back on our learned desire to be entertained. Formative worship will not always be "fun," but what's "fun" is usually not very *counter*formative because it simply confirms our own preferences and reinforces a desire for comfort and familiarity.

So what might a formative youth ministry for liturgical animals look like? No revolution is needed. To the contrary, formative youth ministry grows out of several simple convictions and practices.

First, one of the best decisions we can make for the formation of our children is to enfold them in a congregation that is committed to historic Christian worship *and* multigenerational gathering. If worship is the heart of discipleship, and intentional, historic worship carries the gospel in ways we can never articulate, then youth ministry—like the rest of the Christian life—should be centered in the sanctuary. This means that one of the most important parenting decisions we make is where to worship. Looking for the coolest or most popular youth group might not be the best indicator of where our children will be conformed to the image of Christ. To the contrary, it might be a "boring" congregation that actually does more to shape their loves and longing precisely by rehearsing the biblical story, week in and week out, in practices that are at work on their hearts even if they don't realize it. (There can be a certain virtue to "going through the motions.") A congregation committed to the faith formation of young people is one that invites them from an early age to be true worshipers, enfolding and involving them in the congregation's common practice of worship. Young Christians are nourished like all Christians: by the ordinary means of grace offered in the Word and at the Table, in proclamation and sacraments.[7] Formative youth ministry isn't its own thing; it is, rather, the same repertoire of practices that characterize lifelong Christian discipleship. If we're worried about "keeping" young people in the faith, then instead of sequestering young people elsewhere in the building, we should be keeping them with us in the sanctuary.

Second, formative youth ministry will invite young people into a wider repertoire of Christian disciplines as rhythms of the Spirit. As we heard from Craig Dykstra earlier, Christian faith is "the practice of many practices"—not because faith is works but precisely because such practices and disciplines are "habitations of the Spirit."[8] To be introduced to such disciplines is to be given on-ramps into the Spirit's power. Or, in a different metaphor, introducing young people to ancient disciplines of prayer, attention, discernment, fasting, and worship is like giving them rafts to make their way into the river of grace. This is the conviction behind the Valparaiso Project's teen curriculum, *Way to Live*.[9] Instead of reducing Christianity to a set of ideas—or worse, a set of "don'ts"—this approach to youth ministry invites young people into the ancient practices of the faith. If sanctification is "putting on" Christ, then effective youth ministry invites young people into the practices that are ways of "trying on" Jesus. As such, it must also invite young people to see formative worship as the heart of discipleship.

Finally, formative youth ministry eschews entertainment for service. Forms of youth ministry that tend toward the entertainment model face challenges related to class: the sorts of activities that keep young people entertained are often highly relative to cultural, socioeconomic, and even racial preferences. What sounds like "fun" to one group will be alienating for another; or the sorts of experiences expected by one group might be fiscally out of reach for another. As a result, an unstated focus on entertainment can contribute to an unintended segregation along various lines. And in any case, the unarticulated focus on entertainment only serves to reinforce a wider cultural focus on self that is cultivated by social media. Shouldn't church be the place where we *un*learn such narcissism?

In contrast, service to others can have a kind of leveling effect. No matter how wealthy or privileged, disadvantaged or marginalized, in fact all of us are called to love our neighbor. But more importantly, service has a formative effect: it blunts our cultural practices of self-consciousness and self-regarding, pulling us out of the swirling eddies of our narcissism to an other-regarding

Notre Dame sociologist Christian Smith oversees the monumental National Study of Youth and Religion,[a] an ongoing study of youth spirituality and religious involvement. The findings of this study are both unsettling and insightful. One of the findings is germane to our point concerning multigenerational worship and congregational life. First, despite caricatures and stereotypes, US teenagers who retain and grow in their faith are most significantly influenced by their parents. But there is a crucial second tier of relationships in their formation: nonfamilial adults who encourage them and speak into their lives. Those religiously serious teens they call "The Devoted . . . have a larger number of nonparental adults in their lives whom they can turn to for support, advice, and help. Moreover, the parents of the more religiously serious teens are more likely to know more of the **supportive adults** in their teen children's lives well enough to talk to them, expanding what sociologists call 'network closure' around religious teens. . . . In sum, the lives of more religious teens are, compared to less religious teens, statistically more likely . . . to be linked to and surrounded by adults, particularly nonparental adults who know and care about them and who themselves have social ties to the teens' parents."[b]

a. http://youthandreligion.nd.edu/.
b. Christian Smith, *Soul Searching: The Religious and Spiritual Lives of American Teenagers*, with Melinda Lundquist Denton (New York: Oxford University Press, 2005), 226–27.

concern.[10] Formative youth ministry will be ministry *by* youth rather than just ministry *to* youth.

Schooling the Imagination

A number of these intuitions can also spill over into K–12 classrooms, especially in Christian schools and homeschooling contexts. If liturgies are formative, that means they are implicit pedagogies or teaching strategies that can be marshaled in learning environments beyond the walls of the church.[11] This reframes the goal and task of Christian education so that it's not only a matter of teaching students *about* the faith, nor is it merely a matter of teaching them to *think* about the world from a "Christian perspective." A holistic Christian education does both of these things but also aims to habituate students in the faith, seeing the school as an extended opportunity to create a learning environment that is not just informative but formative. A holistic Christian learning environment doesn't just fill the intellect; it fuels the imagination.

This requires serious intentionality not just about curriculum and content but about pedagogy and teaching strategy. My friends Darryl De Boer, Doug Monsma, and others associated with the Prairie Centre for Education in Alberta have been developing resources that aim to do exactly this. Their program, Teaching for Transformation (TfT), emerged in response to the question that animates this book: What if education weren't first and foremost about what we *know* but about what we *love*? Now used by over fifty schools worldwide, the program enables teachers to create a "know-how" education, an education that shapes the desires of students and teachers.[12]

Teaching for Transformation emphasizes that every unit and every learning experience "needs to immerse students in a story: *the* Story," as De Boer puts it. He summarizes the idea this way: "Teaching for Transformation uses the story discovered in each unit of study to create a powerful and compelling image of God's story, and through that, the nature and character of God; furthermore, TfT invites students to imagine their place in God's story by providing opportunities to practice living the story. Practically, each student and teacher will begin to create a personal 'storyline' and articulate how they see themselves living in God's epic drama." Each day, students are welcomed into classrooms that are intentionally animated by the goal of inviting students into a better story.

What difference does this make for *how* we teach? There is no compromise on content or curriculum. Instead, the content is reframed by being embedded in this narrative framework that invites students to connect their learning with living out the character that God has called them to be (recall our discussion in chapter 4 of how worship "character-izes" us). "It is much more than just passively receiving information within the context of a story," De Boer emphasizes. Students are "activated into" these stories through opportunities to practice what they're learning. Such habit-forming practices are bent on shaping them into "a peculiar people."

Teaching for Transformation does this by identifying a number of biblical "through-lines"—threads of the biblical narrative that wind throughout Scripture and invite us to keep playing them out. These through-lines are roles we are called to play as God's image bearers in a good but broken world. We are called to be, for example, Creation Enjoyers, Idolatry Discerners, Order Discoverers, Beauty Creators. And in all of these God calls us to be God Worshipers and Image Reflectors. How does this look in practice? Consider a brief case study from the experience of a sixth-grade student:

> First, imagine this student learning about supply and demand and loans in an economics unit in a typical classroom. They would learn definitions, see examples of the concepts in action, and, perhaps, participate in some sort of financial simulation; because it involves ideas around money, you can imagine a high level of engagement. Ultimately, the telos of the unit for this student is to score well on the test and eventually, upon graduation, to make wise financial decisions, with the dream that they will be able to make a lot of money one day.
>
> Now imagine this same student learning about economics in a classroom that explicitly has a storyline of "An invitation to a better story," and this student has a starting perspective that there is an inherent brokenness with economics and knowing that they have a role in building God's kingdom by restoring the brokenness of economics. The teacher selects the through-lines of justice seeking and idolatry discerning as the habits they will practice during the learning around supply and demand and loans. Within this context, the telos shifts from making a lot of money one day to the formation of a peculiar person who learns economics as a justice seeker and idolatry discerner.

"It is no surprise," De Boer notes, "that TfT teachers often find that students ultimately absorb the 'what' of the unit better because they have a meaningful story *for* learning."

But we're not even done yet. "Now it is time for the student to grab the cat by the tail," De Boer says with a grin. Teaching the "story" can still be done for brains-on-a-stick, he warns. Thus TfT classrooms provide opportunities for students "to do real work that meets a real need for a real audience." So let's go back to the sixth-grade classroom studying economics.

> Miss Zuidhof wanted the students to learn about the importance of loans. The challenge to the students: how can we use loans to generate money to provide a loan to someone in a developing country? The class transformed into a company, brainstormed and decided that they would do an ice cream sale at school to generate money. So, all the students were tasked with taking out a loan themselves (not from a relative!) in which they could pool their money and purchase the ice cream. So, at this point, everyone in their company is in debt, and they have invested their money elsewhere; students have moved beyond a brain-based learning experience into a *kardia* learning experience. Decisions, all made by the students, like how much to sell their ice cream for, when to sell, and how to advertise, were debated, finalized and executed on a sunny, hot day. From their sales, each student was able to pay off their debt with enough money left over for them to generate a loan for Kiva to use. Kiva (www.kiva.org) is a nonprofit organization that wants to alleviate poverty by making micro loans available. As a class, they decided that they wanted to support a farmer in Guatemala who needed the loan to purchase the supplies needed to grow his crop. Formational learning experiences in TfT invite the students to do real work that meets a real need for a real audience.

Here is learning that reaches the *kardia*, learning that both equips students to think about the world and forms the habits of those called to love the world.

Teaching and learning that are attuned to the spiritual power of habit recognize the cumulative power of little things, the formative power of micro practices. Little things repeated over time in community have a formative effect (why do you think US public schools begin each day with their own version of a creed, the Pledge of Allegiance?). As Winnie the Pooh once said, "Sometimes the smallest things take up the most room in your heart."

Reforming the Formers: On Teaching for Formation

I became a better teacher as soon as I was willing to be a heretic.

Now, before you get worried, let me explain. Something is a heresy only in relation to some orthodoxy. And as a teacher, particularly in higher education, I had been inculcated into an orthodoxy about teaching: under no circumstances should I impose on the autonomy and independence of my students (whose primary goal in life was to become prodigious consumers).

This may seem strange to you, and I mean absolutely no disrespect to my students, but I didn't really know how to teach until it gradually dawned on me that students are *children*. I had basically imagined, early on in my teaching career, that the eighteen-year-olds in my Intro to Philosophy class were graduate-students-in-waiting and that my job was simply to "facilitate" their own theorizing. But as my own children grew and started to look more and more like the students in my classes, it finally hit me: the paradigm for teaching that I absorbed in graduate school was disastrous when it came to actually *teaching* young people. The notion of teaching that I had imbibed was actually allergic to *form*ation, to the notion that I might have a sense of what students *ought* to be. So the "heresy" I began to entertain was a historic notion of the faculty *in loco parentis* ("in place of parents"). I was a heretic precisely because I started to entertain the thought that good teaching might actually be paternalistic. In the environs of educational progressivism, this would be seen as just plain *loco*.

So I came to see that an education that was going to be more intentionally formative would have to push back on some common assumptions of "public" education. More importantly, I came to see that this way of educating for formation points to the higher calling of the teacher—nothing less than forming students as people of *virtue*. Since education is a formative project, aimed at the Good, the True, and the Beautiful, then the teacher is a steward of transcendence who needs not only to *know* the Good but also to teach from that conviction. The teacher of virtue will not apologize for seeking to apprentice students to the Good, the True, and the Beautiful. But she will also run up against the scariest aspect of this: that virtue is often absorbed from exemplars.

If we are going to be formative teachers, we need to reflect critically on our own formation as teachers. Our own educations—particularly for those who have gone through the intense secular "novitiate" that is graduate school—were also formations. But we often don't realize the extent to which we absorbed a very different story about the *telos* of learning that continues to operate in our unconscious. So we need to ask ourselves: What are our society's default assumptions about the ends and goals of education? What visions and values about education have we absorbed in the course of our own university educations?

If we analyzed this, I think we'd find that implicit in the dominant models of education is a modern, secularist narrative that prizes *autonomy* as the ultimate good. Thus the goal of education is reduced to "critical thinking," which only turns out to be an empty, vacuous way of saying that education will simply enable young people to choose whatever "good" they see fit. In this picture, "freedom" requires the loss of a *telos*, since any stipulation of "the Good" impinges on the autonomy of the individual. In other words, such a model of education actually precludes *virtue*.

We need to appreciate how far this departs from a classical education in virtue and from a "thick" notion of Christian formation. As James Davison Hunter puts it in his brilliant analysis *The Death of Character*, "There have never been 'generic' values."[13] Virtues are thick realities tethered to particular communities governed by a particular Story. An education in virtue, then, will have to resist the regnant orthodoxy we often absorb in our own formal educations. But we also need to recognize that such notions of autonomy and independence are absorbed through *in*formal educations, through the continuing education, so to speak, that is effected by our immersion in the secular liturgies of Americanism.

So if education is going to be formative—and more specifically, form students in the Christian faith—we first need to re-form the formers. If we, as educators, are going to be part of a classical project of education that seeks to form the whole person, to apprentice students to a love for the Good, the True, and the Beautiful as revealed to us in Christ, then *we* need to be *re*formed and *trans*formed. Educational reform, you might say, begins with us.

I spend a lot of time on airplanes. The rituals of flight have become second nature for me. When the cabin door closes, I shut down my phone, pick up my *New Yorker*, and tune out the drone of the crew as they enumerate all the safety procedures we will allegedly perform with aplomb in the event that our plane begins plummeting toward earth.

But recently I heard a rote part of the flight attendant's script as if for the first time. No doubt this will sound familiar:

> Oxygen and the air pressure are always being monitored. In the event of loss of cabin pressure, an oxygen mask will automatically appear in front of you. To start the flow of oxygen, pull the mask towards you. Place it firmly over your nose and mouth, secure the elastic band behind your head, and breathe normally. Although the bag does not inflate, oxygen is flowing to the mask. If you are traveling with a child or someone who requires assistance, secure your own mask first, and then assist the other person. Keep your mask on until a uniformed crew member advises you to remove it.

There's an interesting principle here that might have a much wider scope. In the event of an emergency, if I am going to be able to help my neighbors, I first need to put on my own oxygen mask.

If I'm going to be *able* to help the child beside me to secure her oxygen mask, I need to first secure my own.

Similarly, if I am going to be a teacher of virtue, I need to be a virtuous teacher. If I hope to invite students into a formative educational project, then I, too, need to relinquish any myth of independence, autonomy, and self-sufficiency and recognize that my own formation is never final. Virtue is not a one-time accomplishment; it requires a *maintenance* program. So how can educators of virtue be *re*formed and *trans*formed? What practices can sustain such a lofty pedagogical project?

Recognizing that Jesus gave the gift of his Spirit, who is our continuing teacher, we should also recognize that the Spirit gives us the gift of practices that are "habitations of the Spirit," conduits of grace and illumination. Let me describe just a few.

First, we can begin by seeing worship as a kind of "faculty development." Just by committing ourselves to communities of formative Christian worship, we are refueling our own imaginations with the biblical story, immersing our own hearts in the reconciling practices of the body of Christ. This is one of the most important commitments we can make if we hope to be formative teachers: to submit ourselves to the disciplines of Christian worship.

Second, we can cultivate practices of faculty "life together," as Bonhoeffer put it. Like the stonemasons we encountered in Wenger's story in chapter 5, we Christian teachers sometimes have to be reminded, amid the workaday pressures of class prep and grading, that we are building cathedrals. One of the most important practices we can undertake as Christian educators is to cultivate time and space to *re*narrate to one another just what we're doing together. Reminding one another of that is a huge part of sustaining the ethos of our institutions—a reminder that we aren't just grading math tests; we're building prime citizens of the coming kingdom of God. Every school community needs to foster an ethos of mutual renarration. Let me then suggest a few *communal* practices for reforming the formers:

1. *Eat together.* Don't underestimate the ethos that is fostered by sharing a table.
2. *Pray together.* More specifically, pray together in ways that are *formative.* Pray the Psalms; pray the Divine Office; inhabit the rhythms of the liturgical year and the narrative sweep of Scripture in prayer. You might also find this is an opportunity to *confess* to one another.
3. *Sing together.* The bodily blending of voices has important, unarticulated implications for cultivating harmony in your community. Theologian and musician Steven Guthrie points out that we learn something about submission when we sing. "What kind of mutual submission happens in song?" he asks. "For one thing, singing words together involves synchronicity—staying in time with one another. The singers submit themselves to a common tempo, a common musical structure and rhythm."[14] Singing together is a way for a staff to practice harmony, mutual submission, and the synchronicity needed for the shared mission of Christian education.
4. *Think and read together.* Discuss the substance of your common work and vocation as educators instead of just gathering to deal with "business." Visit one another's classes and provide honest, constructive feedback. My friend Matt Beimers, a Christian school principal in Surrey, British Columbia, would add to the list: play together, grieve together, listen to one another's stories. This vision of education is communal.

Finally, undertake practices *for* students as a teacher. Don't underestimate how cultivating loving concern for your students can itself be a (re)formative experience. I experienced something like this several years ago when I taught an advanced seminar on phenomenology and cognitive science at 8:30 in the morning. This was incredibly challenging material to consider at such an early hour, so I made a promise to my students: I went to the local Goodwill store, bought a cheap coffee maker, and promised them that I would always have coffee ready and waiting for them by 8:25 a.m. each day. That way they could roll out of bed, pull on some sweatpants and a cap, and not have to worry about finding their caffeine fix before class: it would be ready and waiting for them here. Since the course was specifically focused on aspects of embodiment, this was a way of honoring their own embodiment.

But I hadn't anticipated an unintended consequence of this seemingly banal routine. Over the course of the semester, I found that the simple practice of having to prepare the coffee ahead of time also meant that I started anticipating the students' arrival in more intentional ways. Instead of cramming to prepare my notes I could focus on creating a space for the students to be welcomed into, fresh with the scent of brewing coffee, a kind of incense for early-morning learning. In the process, I found my own attention shifted from self-regard to concern for the students. And in the moments it took to make the coffee, I would silently pray for the students, anticipating their arrival and the challenges of that day's material, recalling some personal struggles students had shared. The simple act of making coffee became its own little ritual of contemplation and prayer, a habit of pedagogical hospitality.[15] What started as a promise to do something simple, tangible, and embodied became an incubator of virtue.

Teachers of virtue are not born; they are *formed*. They are not "produced" by a diploma or merely credentialed by a certificate; they are *shaped* by immersion in practices that bend their loves and longing toward Christ and his coming kingdom. In short, becoming a teacher of virtue takes practice.

Rites of Passage

If liturgies are pedagogies of desire, then this model has implications for every level of education, from K–12 up through college or university and on into seminary and graduate school. Teasing this out was, in fact, the central focus of *Desiring the Kingdom*—a picture further supplemented in *Teaching and Christian Practices*[16]—so I won't repeat those implications here.

However, we might consider just one facet of what a liturgical paradigm means for education. (I'll draw on examples from higher education, but you might be able to imagine analogues at lower levels.) If we shift the sole focus of education from the dissemination of information to an emphasis on holistic formation, we will need to zoom out, as it were, and consider education within a wider purview. In particular, we will need to be attentive to the *telos* of education: To what end are we educating students? What we teach is important, but *why* we want students to learn is equally important. Helping students gain this teleological purview is part of the project of a holistic, formative education, especially at the college level. While Christian understandings of education that emphasize the notion of "worldview" affirm that every sphere and discipline is a relevant area of study, a liturgical paradigm invites us to ask new questions about the implications of our education. What are we going to *do* with it? This is not a merely instrumental, pragmatic question ("So what?"), and even less a crass economic concern ("How much will I make with this major?"). To the contrary, the *telos* question is about ultimate ends, and thus ultimately about our loves. While I can absolutely be an engineer or musician or financial analyst "to the glory of God," I need to consider the ultimate ends to which my work is going to be oriented. A Christian education can never be merely a mastery of a field of knowledge or technical skills; learning is embedded in a wider vision of who I am called to be and what God is calling the world to be. How does *my* learning fit in this Story? And what practices will cultivate this *ultimate* orientation in me?

Cultivating a teleological perspective on education can also provide a critical purview from which we can evaluate a university education. Every education has a *telos*; it's just that "secular" or public education either pretends not to have one or pretends that the end of education is wholly pragmatic (i.e., credentialing for a job so one can earn an increased income and thereby purchase consumer goods). But an implicit *telos* can sometimes be all the more formative precisely because we don't realize we're being formed (recall our discussion about unconscious automations in chapter 2). Zooming out to consider the ultimate *telos* of education—the story that nourishes the university project—is a way to make explicit what is otherwise implicit.

This holistic, formative approach to education, then, is bound up with a teleological purview—embedding the tasks of teaching and learning in a bigger vision and ultimate Story that guide and govern learning. As such, the ways we "frame" learning can themselves be formative, reinforcing a broader, ultimate vision. Every community of practice has "gateways" into it, and every space within that community has its own mini frames and micro gateways that "set up" what we're doing together. These are what I'd like to call "framing" practices. Whether you're starting high school athletics or joining a corporation or becoming a member of the art museum, every "culture" or community of practice has rituals of orientation and repetition that reinforce the mission, goals, and ethos of the organization. And the best—that is, most formative—rituals of orientation and development do so in ways that work on the imagination and don't just inform the intellect. (The absolute worst corporate orientations are PowerPoint slide after PowerPoint slide of data and rules and information that never come close to touching the imagination.) Formative framing practices invite us to become participants in a story and find tactile, aesthetic ways to keep reorienting us in that story. There are *macro* framing practices that are gateways to a new community, often bound up with our initial orientation to a community of practice; and then there are *micro* framing practices that are more like daily, repeated routines and rituals that keep reinforcing the bigger vision announced at orientation. (This distinction could also be described as the distinction between "momentous" and "mundane" framing practices.)

For example, consider a student who is joining the high school football team. At the very beginning, before the student ever laces up his cleats for practice, both the player and parents will be invited to perhaps several orientation meetings that not only lay out the nitty-gritty logistics but also articulate the veritable "culture" of the team—the goals, expectations, vision, and so forth. That big vision then gets reinforced by all sorts of day-to-day routines and rituals—from cheers and chants to posters in the locker room to veritable sermonettes from the coach to social cues and expectations. You don't just join the West Dillon football team; you *become* an West Dillon Panther ("Clear eyes, full hearts, can't lose"). While 95 percent of the time the team might look the same as any other high school football team, in fact it is these framing practices that cultivate the unique culture of each team. While the framing practices take up little time, they have disproportionate influence on the ethos of the team—and hence on the formation of team members.

Consider, then, the sorts of framing practices that characterize higher education. What do students learn in the week before their college classes ever start? What stories are absorbed in the practices of orientation and Frosh Week? What sorts of identities are cultivated in the framing practices of football games and final exam weeks? What do these tell us the university is *for*? What Story is framing the work of learning in laboratories and lecture halls?

While these can be critical questions in evaluating any form of higher education, they are also opportunities for Christian colleges and universities to be more intentional about framing teaching and learning so as to reinforce the *telos* of higher education. Our macro/micro (momentous/mundane) framing practices send important and (disproportionately) influential signals about *why* we are learning. This is an opportunity for Christian colleges and universities (and for campus ministries at public or "secular" universities). Instead of thinking primarily about the ideas we want students to be informed with, we should be thinking about the *rites* of initiation and inculcation into the community of practice that is the university.

The framing rites for higher learning can extend the practices of worship and reinforce how our learning is an extension of the mission of the church while also locating the task of Christian higher education within the Story of the gospel. And again, there are both macro and micro versions of such framing rituals.

On a macro or momentous level, we should be intentional about the rites of orientation (and commencement, the *sending* or *missio* moment of higher ed). Consider just two tangible examples of rituals in which our own children participated as part of their orientation process at a Christian university. The first was a worship service in which students and parents were invited to inhabit the biblical story in a way that echoes the gathering of the body of Christ every Sunday. This was a liturgical bridge between the church and college. The worship service rehearsed the covenant faithfulness of God, reminding us all that the same God who has been faithful throughout childhood is the gracious Lord who reigns over the university. This culminated in a powerful, tactile ritual laden with metaphorical significance. Each family—student and parents and siblings together—was invited to the front of the sanctuary. Placed around the Communion table were baptismal fonts filled with water. Each family was invited to dip their hands into the waters of baptism, to stir the memories of our own baptisms and thus recall the promises made—by God, by families, by the church—to see each child of God come to the fullness of maturity in Christ. And so we could release our children into this learning community with a tangible reminder of God's unwavering faithfulness, and students could venture into this new season of life, their hands dripping with the grace of the sacrament. Here was a community of learning embedded in the covenant of grace.

This was also the occasion for farewell between student and parents. Tearfully we said our good-byes, but with confidence and hope. The next day, the students were invited into another tangible ritual of orientation. In a way that met both their fears and their hopes—and their natural inclinations as liturgical animals—each student was given a candle with a cupcake-like holder made of paper. On the paper they were invited to write something they needed to leave behind. Coming to learn in a community that worships a gracious God of second (and third and fourth and . . .) chances, the students were encouraged to embrace the grace of this new beginning by casting their cares upon the One who cares for them. On the piece of paper they could write a sin they needed to leave behind, or a fear they wanted to overcome, or a trauma they hoped to be delivered from. Embedding this exercise in a rich context of prayer and praise, these notes became enchanted in a way—they carried a significance beyond their materiality. Each student was invited to wrap her note around the candle and then cast it adrift on the campus pond, relinquishing the concern to the care of God the Father. In the dark of the final night before classes began, hundreds of fears (and hopes) covered by the light of grace floated across the pond, into the darkness on the other side. Tomorrow, the students themselves would set sail on a new adventure of learning.

Contextualizing Christian higher education in the ultimate context of a kingdom-*telos* invites an array of practices in areas from admissions through orientation and even commencement and alumni relations—practices that rehearse the story of God's renewal of all things not just *in*formationally but *form*ationally.

There are also ample opportunities to embody this on a micro level. The formative significance of framing practices can give us a new appreciation for how worship practices "sanctify" classrooms and laboratories and other learning spaces—not because a little prayer thereby "Christianizes" whatever we're teaching but rather because even an integrated curriculum needs to be wed to practices that "carry" an understanding of Christian faith that can never be articulated on a syllabus. When we move from an expressivist to a formative framework, the habit of opening prayer in a college classroom can become a powerful ongoing practice that centers and situates learning within the sweep of God's reconciliation of all things. If Christ is the wisdom of God and Christian higher education is the pursuit of wisdom, then how could we not submit our teaching and learning to the discipline of prayer? Consider, for example, this prayer of St. Thomas Aquinas:

Ante Studium
A Prayer before Study

Ineffable Creator,
Who, from the treasures of Your wisdom,
has established three hierarchies of angels,
has arrayed them in marvelous order
above the fiery heavens,
and has marshaled the regions
of the universe with such artful skill,

You are proclaimed
the true font of light and wisdom,
and the primal origin
raised high beyond all things.

Pour forth a ray of Your brightness
into the darkened places of my mind;
disperse from my soul
the twofold darkness
into which I was born:
sin and ignorance.

You make eloquent the tongues of infants.
Refine my speech
and pour forth upon my lips
the goodness of Your blessing.

Grant to me
keenness of mind,
capacity to remember,
skill in learning,
subtlety to interpret,
and eloquence in speech.

May You
guide the beginning of my work,
direct its progress,
and bring it to completion.

You Who are true God and true Man,
Who live and reign, world without end.
Amen.[17]

But framing prayer need not be only for wisdom and illumination and study. We can also situate the classroom in the wider
world. Opening prayers can be a way to invite students beyond the
bubble of the campus. In the spirit of the "prayers of the people,"
our opening or framing prayers can invite students from the space
of leisure and privilege that is the college classroom to remember
those who are suffering around the world or down the street. On a
cold winter morning, before an economics class discusses macro-
economic policy and poverty, a prayer for the homeless enduring a
frigid cold snap can recontextualize what would be an otherwise
abstract discussion, once again indexing our teaching and learning
to the biblical hunger for *shalom*. An international relations class
can be formatively framed when opened with prayers from the
global south. When a philosophy class dealing with the problem of
evil is bookended with the responsive prayer of psalms of lament,
students are not just invited to think about an abstract "problem";
they are invited into a story, one that reminds us that these same
prayers of lament were prayed by the incarnate Son of God. This
is how we learn by heart; this is how the heart learns to love.

7

YOU MAKE WHAT YOU WANT

Vocational Liturgies

Everything Matters

The biblical doctrine of creation is not just about where we came from; it's about where we are. It's not just about who we are, but whose we are. It's not just a statement about our past; it is a calling to a future.

We are not just dawdling around in some anonymous cosmos; we are *home*. We are dwelling in God's world. This isn't just "nature"; it is *creation*.[1] And it is "very good" (Gen. 1:31). The material creation is not just some detour from our heavenly existence. It is the very good abode created by our heavenly Father. Creation is not some icky, regrettable mistake on God's part. It is the product of his *love*.

Some Christians seem to think otherwise. Some Christians try to be holier than God when it comes to creation, seeing it only as the world "under the control of the evil one" (1 John 5:19). And so, with their escape pods prepared, ready and eager to abandon creation, they're convinced that God doesn't really care about it either. But that's hardly God's take on creation. Indeed, in the incarnation, the Word becomes flesh, the Creator of the universe moves into our neighborhood. The infinite, transcendent God becomes embodied like us. And notice how the whole Story ends in Revelation 21: God doesn't eject us from creation; he comes down to dwell with us in a new creation.[2] So the end of the Story confirms the beginning: creation is very good. While we also need to appreciate how God's creation has been marred and broken, and how God is renewing and restoring it, throughout the Story God continues to confirm this evaluation: creation is very good.

That's why everything matters. To understand the world as God's creation is to hear rumbling in the world itself a *calling*. When the Spirit gives you ears to hear and eyes to see, creation is a gift that calls—it is a chamber of God's glory that resonates with an *invitation*.

Your (Com)mission (Should You Choose to Accept It)

The doctrine of creation is not just a metaphysics—a statement of what the cosmos *is*. Rather, think of the biblical theology of creation as a *manifesto*, as marching orders, as a commission. More importantly, the biblical teaching on creation is a charge, a *mission*, a commission that sends us into God's good but broken world with a *calling*. We can summarize this (com)mission in three verbs: image, unfold, and occupy. These are "do" words, action terms. Let me unpack each of these elements in a little more detail.

First, you are called to *image God*. We are created in the image of God (Gen. 1:27). But I think it's important to hear this more as a verb than a noun—as a task and mission rather than a property or characteristic. The "image of God" (*imago Dei*) is not some de facto property of *homo sapiens* (whether will or reason or language, or what have you); rather, the image of God is a *task*, a *mission*. As Richard Middleton comments in his book *The Liberating Image*, "The *imago Dei* designates the royal office or calling of human beings as God's representatives and agents in the world, granted authorized power to share in God's rule or administration of the earth's resources and creatures." We are commissioned as God's image bearers, his vice-regents, charged with the task of "ruling" and caring for creation, which includes the task of cultivating it, unfolding and unfurling its latent possibilities through human making—in short, through *culture*. "Imaging God," Middleton points out, "thus involves representing and perhaps extending in some way God's rule on earth through ordinary communal practices of human sociocultural life."[3]

Do you know what that means? We *image* God in our work—in all of the very earthly and human, all-too-human things we are called to do.

Second, you are called to *unfold creation's potential*. Notice in Genesis 1:28–30 that our task as image bearers is to be fruitful and multiply (the fun part!), to "cultivate" the earth, and to "have dominion" over creation. Creation is indeed very good, but that doesn't mean that it is *complete*. Creation doesn't come into existence with schools and art museums and iPhones and automobiles. God places us in creation with an invitation to unpack and unfurl all of the latent potential that God has folded into creation—and commissions us to do just that. As Tolkien puts it, we are "sub-creators."[4]

Now there are *norms* for that: we can either do this well or do this badly. In a sense, the criterion for "good unfolding" is the biblical vision of that coming city. In other words, the consummation of the Story in Scripture reveals to us what God wants for his creation. God's desires for creation—the *shalom* and flourishing that are painted in those pictures of the kingdom—are clues as to how we should be unfolding the latent potential of creation. This is why we need to be attentive to how *our* desires become aligned with God's desires. As I've been trying to show, this isn't just a matter of information; it's a matter of habit-formation.

It's also why we need to beware of monsters: our creational impulse can turn into Promethean striving. Our cultural creations can outstrip us, even at times when the culture-making impulse is suffused with the best of intentions. And so we need to appreciate that culture is not neutral or benign—it is not simply a "good." More importantly, we need to remember that creation—especially *our* creations—does something *to* us. So a biblical theology of creation, while affirming the goodness of creation and the goodness of our culture-making impulse, also comes with a radical caution. We must say, "Yes, *but . . .*"

Finally, you are called to *occupy creation*. To take up our commission today—to carry out the work of being God's image bearers—requires attesting to the fact that something is wrong. It requires recognizing that we're not in Kansas anymore—we're not in the Garden anymore. And so the body of Christ is called to be that peculiar people who occupy creation and remind the world that it belongs to God.

The body of Christ should be a testimony to the kingdom that is coming, bearing witness to how the world will be otherwise. Our work and our practices should be foretastes of that coming new city and thus should include protest and critique. Our engagement with God's world is not about running the show or winning a culture war. We are called to be witnesses, not necessarily winners. We are called to what James Davison Hunter has aptly described as "faithful presence."[5] Faithful presence is how we occupy creation.

This requires being regularly recentered in the Story. And so we "occupy" creation in that motley tent camp that is the church. Yes, God's affirmation of the goodness of creation tells us that everything matters; and you will learn that over and over again *in the church*. It is in the worship of the Triune God that we are restored by being restoried. It is the practices of Christian worship

A reminiscence from British architect Patrick Lynch on work, love, and the relation between the two:

My father was what is known as a "small builder," which means that he undertook small domestic projects in the main, building extensions to large Victorian houses along the River Thames at Henley. Only once did he build a new house. Sometimes he just repaired and amended old walls. He was principally a bricklayer in a period when this was a common and well-respected trade, although he was apprenticed as a surveyor and trained at night school to achieve his OND certificates. But office life bored my father and he longed for outdoor work and the independence of his own building projects, and so he fell back upon skills learnt from his stepfather, and used these alongside his draughting skills to gain planning consents for small projects which he subsequently built. In a rather obvious way, looking back, my brother and I fulfilled an unspoken ambition on behalf of our family, and we became architects. I guess **bricks smelt of love and hope** to us.[a]

a. Patrick Lynch, "Brick Love," in *Common Ground: A Critical Reader*, ed. David Chipperfield, Kieran Long, and Shumi Bose (Venezia, Italy: Marsilio Editori, 2012), 121.

that renarrate our imagination so that we can perceive the world *as* God's creation and thus hear his *call* that echoes within it.

This now intersects with our core theme because our (culture-) making, our work, is generated as much by what we *want* as by what we believe. We are made to be makers, but as makers we remain lovers. So if you are what you love, then you *make* what you love. Your cultural labor—whether in finance or fine arts, as a fireman or a first-grade teacher—is animated less by "principles" that you carry in your head and more by habits of desire that operate under the hood of consciousness.

This was illustrated for me recently while reading about the unfolding drama of the *Star Wars* films. In a creative review of Chris Taylor's book *How Star Wars Conquered the Universe*, Cass Sunstein focuses on a crucial turning point in the years-long development of the story—what he calls the "I am your father" moment when Darth Vader reveals to Luke Skywalker their relationship. This crucial plot twist in *The Empire Strikes Back* effectively transformed even the movie that came before it: it was a creative moment that had retroactive effects. But what's most fascinating is that, despite George Lucas's own claims to the contrary,[6] evidence shows that he, the creator of the story, didn't know at the beginning that the plot would take this turn. "Lucas decided only at a relatively late stage," Sunstein comments, "that Darth Vader is Luke's father." Sunstein recounts the creative context reconstructed by Taylor: "While writing the climactic scene of *The Empire Strikes Back*, Lucas decided that Vader should say to Luke, 'We will rule the galaxy as father and son.' Those words apparently jarred his imagination, producing what must have been an 'aha,' a shiver, a tingle in the spine, suddenly explaining 'at a strike why everyone from Uncle Owen to Obi-Wan to Yoda has been so concerned about Luke's development, and whether he would grow up to be like his father.'"[7] This narrative, of course, was created by Lucas, but even the creator didn't realize where his own story was headed. This gets at something important about creative processes more generally—and hence tells us something about culture-making. His making and creating were, in a way, governed by impulses at work beyond his own awareness.

Consider, for example, this conversation between Lucas and his collaborator Lawrence Kasdan while writing *Return of the Jedi*:

> KASDAN: I think you should kill Luke and have Leia take over.
> LUCAS: You don't want to kill Luke.
> KASDAN: Okay, then kill Yoda.
> LUCAS: I don't want to kill Yoda. You don't have to kill people. You're a product of the 1980s. You don't go around killing people. It's not nice.
> KASDAN: No, I'm not. I'm trying to give the story some kind of an edge to it. . . .
> LUCAS: By killing somebody, I think you alienate the audience.
> KASDAN: I'm saying that the movie has more emotional weight if someone you love is lost along the way; the journey has more impact.

LUCAS: I don't like that and I don't believe that.

KASDAN: Well, that's all right.

LUCAS: I have always hated that in movies, when you go along and one of the main characters gets killed. This is a fairytale. You want everybody to live happily ever after and nothing bad happens to anybody. . . . The whole point of the film, the whole emotion that I am trying to get at the end of this film, is for you to be real uplifted, emotionally and spiritually, and feel absolutely good about life. That is the greatest thing that we could possibly ever do.

Notice what governs Lucas's creative impulses at this point: what he believes and what he wants. These beliefs and wants and sensibilities are at work under the hood of our conscious awareness. For example, early on it seems that Lucas wanted to inflect the story with a Buddhist theme: that it is attachment that causes evil—that people turn to evil when they can't "let go." But by *Return of the Jedi*, some other story is at work in Lucas's imagination because "Vader is redeemed not by distance but by attachment." Despite Lucas's stated intention, it turns out that Vader "is redeemed by love, not distance." As Sunstein summarizes the point, "Lucas' unconscious mind . . . turned out to be more complicated than his apparent intentions." Indeed, our creative "I am your father" moments "tend to erupt from the unconscious."

Which is why all of us—as culture-makers and meaning-creators—need to curate our unconscious, to be attentive to the formation of our imagination. Whether we're entrepreneurs launching a tech start-up or first-time parents starting a family, our "creative" work as human beings made in God's image is sort of *pulled* out of us by our attraction to a vision of the good life. Our making bubbles up from our imagination, which is fueled by a Story of what flourishing looks like. We all carry some governing Story in our bones that shapes our work more than we might realize because that Story has taught us what to love (and as we emphasized in chapter 2, you might not love what you think because you might not realize what Story has *really* captured your imagination).

If you are what you love, and you make what you want, then we need to be attentive to how our wants are formed if we want to be faithful makers. We need to curate the unconscious, the storehouse of governing stories. Be careful what you worship; it will shape what you want, and therefore what you make and how you work.

Tradition *for* Innovation

Many evangelicals are beginning to affirm this expansive sense of mission and a more holistic theology of creation that affirms not only the Great Commission but also the cultural mandate.[8] As Gabe Lyons documents in *The Next Christians*, evangelicals are bringing an activist piety to a number of different cultural "channels"—from politics and technology to fashion and art. Young evangelicals are energetic social entrepreneurs interested in creativity, invention, and innovation beyond the narrow sphere of the church. They are also intensely interested in addressing matters of justice, oppression, and societal disorder. They want to "restore" a broken world; they want to both make the world anew and put the world to rights.[9] I expect many mainline Christians will be encouraged to see them finally getting on the bandwagon.

On the other hand, evangelicalism continues to be a hotbed of almost unfettered religious innovation, ever confident of its ability to compete in the shifting marketplace of contemporary spirituality. The entrepreneurial independence of evangelical spirituality (which is as old as the American colonies) leaves room for all kinds of congregational start-ups that need little if any institutional support. Catering to more and more specialized niches, these start-ups are not beholden to liturgical forms or institutional legacies. Indeed, many of them confidently announce their desire to "reinvent church."

These are, I want to suggest, competing trajectories. For we cannot hope to restore the world if we are constantly reinventing the church. Let me explain.

The cultural labor of restoration certainly requires imaginative innovation. Good culture-making requires that we imagine the world otherwise—which means seeing *through* the status-quo stories we're told and instead envisioning kingdom come. We need new energy, new strategies, new initiatives, new organizations, even new institutions. If we hope to put the world to rights, we need to think differently and act differently and build institutions that foster such action.

But if our cultural work is going to be *restorative*—if it is going to put the world *to rights*—then we need imaginations that have absorbed a vision for how things ought to be. Our innovation and invention and creativity will need to be bathed in an eschatological vision of what the world is made for, what it's called to be—what the prophets often described as *shalom*. Innovation *for* justice and *shalom* requires that we be regularly immersed in the story of God reconciling all things to himself.

That immersion happens in *worship*—in intentional, historic, liturgical forms that carry the Story in ways that sink into our bones and seep into our unconscious. This is why the unfettered, undisciplined "reinvention" of the church actually undercuts our ability to carry out innovative, restorative culture-making.

Design guru Herbert Simon once observed, "Everyone designs who devises courses of action aimed at changing existing situations into preferred ones."[10] Robert Grudin elucidates this sense of design as intrinsic to the calling of humanity: "Design is the purest exercise of human skill. To add a new instrument or process to the design treasury is to engage in the force of evolving nature."[11] In this sense, good design tells the truth about the world. "A well-designed hoe," Grudin comments, "speaks the truth to the ground that it breaks and, conversely, tells us the truth about the ground."[12] Culture-making more generally is an act of such truth-telling, life-giving design. "Legal and cultural paradigms," for example, "are not normally spoken of as designs, but in fact they are blueprints that sculpt the character of large populations and channel human energies in specific directions. The US Constitution is the design equivalent of the Jaguar XKE and the Palazzo Te: it liberates human energies and maximizes human options."[13]

Humans are made to design. Indeed, if designer Herbert Simon's axiom is correct, then we could rightly say that the gospel itself is a design project—it is the good news that humanity is now liberated to take up the design work given to us at creation, to assume our (co)mission as creation's designers.

And Christian worship, I suggest, is a design studio. The church's mission is to send out innovators and designers whose actions aim "at changing existing situations into preferred ones." But innovators and restorers and makers and designers also need the church to be an imagination station, a space for rehabituating our imagination to the "true story of the whole world." Our imaginations need to be restored, recalibrated, and realigned by an affective immersion in the story of God in Christ reconciling the world to himself. That's what intentional, historic Christian worship does. We need pastors and priests and worship leaders (and teachers and youth pastors and college professors) who appreciate that Christian worship is an imagination station—and that the normativity of the Story needs to be affectively carried in our worship. This is why form matters. Which is just another way of saying that the Christian liturgical *tradition* should be seen as a resource to foster cultural *innovation*.

If the church is going to send out "restorers" who engage culture for the common good, we will need to recover and remember the rich imaginative practices of historic Christian worship that carry the unique story of the gospel. In this way, the liturgical tradition is a fund for the imagination:

- Kneeling in confession and voicing "the things we have done and the things we have left undone" tangibly and viscerally impresses on us the brokenness of our world and should humble our own pretensions.

- Pledging allegiance in the Creed is a *political* act—a reminder that we are citizens of a coming kingdom, curtailing our temptations to overidentify with any configuration of the earthly city.

- The rite of baptism, where the congregation vows to help raise the child and come alongside the parents, is just the liturgical formation we need in order to be a people who can support those raising children with intellectual disabilities or those with the calling and courage to adopt special-needs children.

- Sitting at the Lord's Table with the risen King, where *all* are invited to eat, is a tactile reminder of the just, abundant world that God longs for.

In sum, the innovative, restorative work of culture-making needs to be primed by those liturgical traditions that orient our imagination to kingdom come. In order to foster a Christian imagination, we don't need to *invent*; we need to *remember*. We cannot hope to re-create the world if we are constantly reinventing "church," because we will reinvent ourselves right out of the Story. Liturgical tradition is the platform for imaginative innovation.

The Gift of Constraints

I don't want to pretend this is easy. In many ways, the blank slate of "reinventing the church" is much easier. But it's not a question of what's easy; it's a question of how the Spirit will form our habits, *re*form our imaginations, and *trans*form our hearts. It's only that kind of deep formation of our creative unconscious that will truly generate faithful innovation and cultural creation that bends toward kingdom come.

But let's face it: all of us inhabit institutions—and perhaps especially *churches*—that we would have built otherwise. We are heirs to policies and procedures and physical environments that have aspects we'd happily do without. Sometimes we bristle under the constraints put upon us by founders and historical bodies that could know nothing of our contemporary challenges. All of us have daydreamed about what it would be like to be free of such constraint—to "reimagine" the institution from scratch. *Then*, we tell ourselves, we'd really be free to push forward our mission and vision. But now, in the real world, these constraints are like millstones, anchors dragging on the bottom as we try to steer the ship forward into new waters.

Could we ever imagine receiving such constraints as gifts? Indeed, is it possible that the constraints of handed-down traditions could be catalysts for creativity and imagination?

I was recently struck by something of a parable in this regard. In 2012, after a protracted—and very public—legal battle, the Barnes Foundation opened a new site on museum row in Philadelphia, transporting Albert Barnes's world-class collection of modern art from its former suburban home in Lower Merion, Pennsylvania. The legal wrangling need not detain us here. It's the result that yields an interesting case study of "traditioned innovation."

Martin Filler summarizes the dynamics of the situation in his very helpful overview in the *New York Review of Books*: "Barnes had insisted that none of his eight hundred paintings or thousands of other objects could ever be sold, loaned, or removed from the elaborate installations he contrived for them. Thus, though the court agreed to the relocation, it stipulated that the collector's displays be strictly maintained in the institution's new home."[14]

Talk about constraints! Permission to move the collection didn't just come with strings attached: it came with the sorts of wire cables that hold up the Golden Gate Bridge. You would think that all one could do with such conditions and constraints is simply duplicate the Lower Merion mansion in an urban context. What else could architects do but fall into Vegas-like imitation and mimicry, simply reproducing a facsimile of the original? Indeed, the new museum wouldn't really need creative architects; it would simply need good copyists.

But a funny thing happened on the way to reproduction: the architectural team of Tod Williams and Billie Tsien refused simple repetition. Accepting the constraints of Barnes's bequest, they received them as a catalyst for creativity. Filler describes the result:

> The legal requirement to reproduce the old galleries made many observers fear that this would limit the designers to an exercise in cultural taxidermy, with little scope left for architectural originality. Remarkably, Williams and Tsien found unexpected expressive range within the confines they were bound to observe. In that respect the outcome of this project is dazzling—the new Barnes is infinitely superior to the vast number of museums designed with a completely free hand, and in hindsight, Judge Stanley R. Ott's 2004 ruling that the display must be exactly duplicated seems Solomonic in its wisdom.

In other words, the new Barnes Foundation building is a concrete example of traditioned innovation. The result is stunning, both externally and internally. Receiving the constraints on gallery space and configuration, the architects imagined a new future for the collection. One might say the new building is a "faithful extension" of the original site: taking up what had been handed down, but without simply parroting the original. Williams and Tsien's design is a creative repetition.

The result is illuminating, both literally and figuratively. Visitors (especially at night) are bedazzled by the "Light Box" that sits atop the length of the building, which then fuels a spacious "Light Court" in the interior. The creative admission of light washes over the reproduced galleries. "The most welcome aspect of the new Barnes," Filler notes, "is the veritable visual resurrection" occasioned by the architects' collaboration with lighting designer Paul Marantz. The works are the same; the arrangement is the same; the rooms are the same; and yet it's as if we are seeing some of them for the first time. The architectural innovation recasts the heritage of the building in ways that highlight the

Image ©2015 The Barnes Foundation

The new Barnes Foundation building is a case study of "traditioned innovation."

beauty of these works—just what attracted Mr. Barnes to them in the first place.

Martin Filler notes another example of this mutual interplay between tradition and innovation in this case. In requiring the preservation of the galleries as arranged by Barnes, the designers inherited a stipulated background for all the paintings: an ocher-colored burlap that Barnes designed specifically for the gallery walls. But with the new illumination, we discover that this color is "so harmonious with most of his pictures that one wonders why it is not widely copied elsewhere." What would have previously been begrudged as Barnes's restrictive idiosyncrasies now begin to make sense.

In sum, what might have been debilitating constraints became catalysts for creative innovation, issuing in a new appreciation for the wisdom of the constraints. "Barnes may have been a crank," Filler concludes, "but he was also touched with some kind of genius."

Think of the cranky constraints in your own context. Could it be more creative not to simply wish them away but to receive them as gifts? Is there a genius embedded in those constraints that some imaginative leadership could unveil, leading to new appreciation? Maybe a "completely free hand" is not what we need. Perhaps what we need is good constraints and the imagination to receive them as gifts for innovation. Could we imagine the authority and inheritance of the historic liturgical tradition as just this sort of liberating constraint that will spark creativity and imagination?

In the same way, our daily work might best flourish within the gift of constraint handed down to us in the tradition of the church's worship and the rhythms of the spiritual disciplines. We might find liberation in liturgy and renewal through ritual.

Vocational Liturgies

What are the rituals that start your day? Many of us have adopted daily habits without much reflection. Our morning rituals probably include a cycle of "checking in"—with email, with Facebook, with Twitter, with the *Wall Street Journal*. If Martian anthropologists landed in our office or at our breakfast table, they might read our hunched posture over our phones as a kind of religious devotion to some electronic talisman.

And what if those rituals aren't just something that you do? What if they are also doing something *to* you? What if those rituals are veritable "liturgies" of a sort? What if pursuing God in our vocations requires immersion in rituals that direct our passions?

I can still remember the day I discovered my vocation. I was in the basement of the library at college when I came across copies of a journal called *Faith and Philosophy*, published by the Society of Christian Philosophers. In the first issue, eminent philosopher Alvin Plantinga published a manifesto of sorts, titled "Advice to Christian Philosophers," first given as his inaugural address at the University of Notre Dame.

In this article, Plantinga powerfully articulated that Christians can and should pursue philosophy, why it was important that they do so, and how to do it with Christian integrity. "We who are Christians and propose to be philosophers," he wrote, "must not rest content with being philosophers who happen, incidentally, to be Christians; we must strive to be Christian philosophers. We must therefore pursue our projects with integrity, independence, and Christian boldness."[15]

Plantinga's vision is relevant to all vocations and professions: he paints a picture in which God is invested in every square inch of his creation—not just the church and theology, but also philosophy and physics, law and economics, agriculture and the arts. We ought not to settle for being Christians who happen to be artists, or lawyers who are simply "also" Christians. We should see our vocations as ways to pursue God himself—and, as Plantinga puts it, to do so with "integrity, independence, and Christian boldness." I received Plantinga's words as nothing less than a clarion call to follow the inklings I'd been having. But whenever I considered philosophy as a possible vocation, my teachers would caution me with some variation on the words of Colossians 2:8: "Do not be taken captive by vain philosophy!" But when I read Plantinga, I was captivated by a vision for *Christian* philosophy: that philosophy could be a way of pursuing God.

And philosophy has helped me think about the very notion of "pursuing" God. I was reminded of this while recently teaching Aristotle's *Metaphysics*. While Aristotle is a Greek philosopher who lived several centuries before Christ, he offered one of the first philosophical arguments for the existence of God—what he called "the First Mover." But for Aristotle, to say that God is the "cause" of everything is not just a claim about our *beginning*; it's also a point about our *end*.

You could say God is not just the One who "pushes" us into existence; he is also the One who *pulls* us toward himself. Aristotle said that this "produces motion as being *loved*." In other words, God doesn't simply propel us; he also *attracts* us. We pursue what we *love*.

Aristotle is on to something that is important for a Christian understanding of vocation. It's not just a matter of loving our work; it's about loving our work *for* God. It's pursuing God *in* our work. God provides us the vision that *pulls* our labor toward his kingdom.

And then in his *Nicomachean Ethics,* Aristotle offers another important insight. He emphasizes that virtues are habits that take *practice.* Habits are *acquired* "dispositions" that get woven into our character. And the way we acquire such habits is through *practice* and *repetition*—through "rituals," you might say.

We've already noted the interesting chemical reaction when you put these two ideas together (as Paul does in passages like Col. 3:12–17): *love* is the ultimate virtue. We are to intentionally "clothe ourselves" with love. So the love that attracts us to God is something that grows through practice and repetition, and if we want to pursue God in our vocations, we need to immerse ourselves in rituals and rhythms and practices whereby the love of God seeps into our very character and is woven into not just how we think but *who we are.*

This is one of the reasons why worship is not some escape from "the work week." To the contrary, our worship rituals train our hearts and aim our desires toward God and his kingdom so that, when we are *sent* from worship to take up our work, we do so with a habituated orientation toward the Lover of our souls.

This is also why we need to think about habit-shaping practices— "vocational liturgies," we might call them—that can sustain this

---

The second stanza of "Father, Help Your People" (*Psalter Hymnal,* no. 607):

> Holy is the setting of each room and yard,
> lecture hall and kitchen, office, shop, and ward.
> Holy is the rhythm of our working hours;
> **hallow then our purpose,** energy, and powers.

love throughout the week. This was John Calvin's vision for the city of Geneva: he wanted to see the entire city governed by the rhythms of morning and evening prayer and psalm-singing, not just for monks and "religious" folk but for all of the butchers and bakers and candlestick makers whose work was equally holy.

Let's think creatively about rhythms and rituals and routines that would let the good news sink into us throughout the week. I'm reminded of an investment banker in Manhattan who spearheaded the practice of listening to the public reading of Scripture with his colleagues on Wall Street. Or of teachers who have committed to the practice of morning prayer as a way to frame their daily work. There are all kinds of ways to contextualize vocational liturgies that train us to love the God who pulls us and calls us.

Like the father of the prodigal son, God is already out ahead of us. He runs to the end of the lane to meet us where we are. He gives us the gifts of good rituals so we can practice loving him with heart, soul, mind, and strength. Thankfully, we pursue God *with* God. We love because he first loved us.

BENEDICTION

We shall not cease from exploration
And the end of all our exploring
Will be to arrive where we started
And know the place for the first time.
                —T. S. Eliot, "Little Gidding"

Worship ends with sending: we are gathered by the grace of our (re)creating God in order to become the image bearers he created us to be, precisely so we can be sent into his world as ambassadors of reconciliation (2 Cor. 5:17–20). The God who *is* love reorders our loves, bending our deepest desires back toward himself, so that we might rightly love our neighbors for his sake. The Spirit rehabituates our loves not merely for the sake of renovation but so that we can love even our enemies. This is what we were made for: to love what God loves. Our *telos* brings us back to our beginning. And we were made to be *sent*.

The Orthodox theologian Alexander Schmemann captures this "holy circle," as it were, in a reflection on worship:

The Orthodox liturgy begins with the solemn doxology: "Blessed is the Kingdom of the Father, the Son and the Holy Spirit, now and

ever, and unto ages of ages." From the beginning the destination is announced: the journey is to the Kingdom. This is where we are going—
and not symbolically, but really. In the language of the Bible, which
is *the* language of the Church, to bless the Kingdom is not simply to
acclaim it. It is to declare it to be the goal, the end of all our desires
and interests, of our whole life, the supreme and ultimate value of all
that exists. To bless is to accept in love, and to move toward what is
loved and accepted. The Church thus is the assembly, the gathering of
those to whom the ultimate destination of all life has been revealed
and who have accepted it. This acceptance is expressed in the solemn
answer to the doxology: Amen. It is indeed one of the most important
words in the world, for it expresses the agreement of the Church to
follow Christ in his ascension to His Father, to make this ascension
the destiny of man. It is Christ's gift to us, for only in Him can we
say Amen to God, or rather He himself is our Amen to God and the
Church is an Amen to Christ. Upon this Amen the fate of the human
race is decided. It reveals that the movement toward God has begun.[1]

And so: *Come* to the feast that is worship so that you can *go*,
renewed and rehabituated by the Spirit, and say "Amen" in everything you love.

FOR FURTHER READING

If you read this book and find yourself hungry for more, you'll find a more detailed and in-depth articulation of these themes in my Cultural Liturgies trilogy (the first two of which are noted below). In the hope that this book might be the beginning of a journey, here are some guides to accompany you along the way.

Abernethy, Alexis D., ed. *Worship That Changes Lives: Multidisciplinary and Congregational Perspectives on Spiritual Transformation*. Grand Rapids: Baker Academic, 2008. A multifaceted consideration of the opportunities and challenges for transformative worship.

Bolsinger, Tod. *It Takes a Church to Raise a Christian: How the Community of God Transforms Lives*. Grand Rapids: Brazos, 2004. A case for the church as the center of discipleship.

Brooks, David. *The Road to Character*. New York: Random House, 2015. An accessible, journalistic account of character, virtue formation, and the importance of imitation. Includes powerful profiles of "exemplars" like Augustine, Dorothy Day, Dwight Eisenhower, and more.

Cosper, Mike. *Rhythms of Grace: How the Church's Worship Tells the Story of the Gospel*. Wheaton: Crossway, 2013. Excellent introduction to the "narrative arc" of intentional Christian worship.

Duhigg, Charles. *The Power of Habit: Why We Do What We Do in Life and Business*. New York: Random House, 2014. An accessible account of both ancient wisdom and scientific insight into the significance of habit in the rhythms of our lives.

Labberton, Mark. *The Dangerous Act of Worship: Living God's Call to Justice*. Downers Grove, IL: InterVarsity, 2012. Reminds us that worship ends with *sending*—that worship shapes a peculiar people called to embody God's desire for *shalom*.

Smith, James K. A. *Desiring the Kingdom: Worship, Worldview, and Cultural Formation*. Cultural Liturgies 1. Grand Rapids: Baker Academic, 2009. An in-depth articulation of the model sketched in *You Are What You Love*. Think of it as the "201" version of the argument presented in this book. Chapter 5 includes a detailed "reading" of the Story implicitly embedded in historic Christian worship.

————. *Imagining the Kingdom: How Worship Works*. Cultural Liturgies 2. Grand Rapids: Baker Academic, 2013. Articulates philosophical foundations for a liturgical theology of culture, with special attention to its implication for planning and leading worship.

Webber, Robert. *Ancient-Future Worship: Proclaiming and Enacting God's Narrative*. Grand Rapids: Baker Books, 2008. Makes the case that historic ("ancient") worship is precisely the gift we need for a faithful witness in our postmodern ("future") context. A significant influence on my own thinking.

————. *The Divine Embrace: Recovering the Passionate Spiritual Life*. Grand Rapids: Baker Books, 2006. Takes spirituality out of the closet of privacy and individualism and locates it smack in the middle of friendship and community.

The Worship Sourcebook: A Classic Resource for Today's Church. 2nd ed. Grand Rapids: Faith Alive / Baker Books, 2013. Produced by the Calvin Institute of Christian Worship, its introduction is a jam-packed short course in the theology of worship and formation. Provides an array of historical and contemporary resources for thoughtful, intentional, trinitarian worship that shapes hearts and minds.

ACKNOWLEDGMENTS

I would never have imagined I might write a book like this, but my friends at Brazos and Baker Publishing Group did, and I'm grateful for their invitation and encouragement (and patience!). Thanks especially to my editor—and more importantly, friend—Bob Hosack, who took a bet on me a long time ago. The entire Brazos team has been incredibly supportive. It's an honor to partner with them. I look forward to our future together.

This book is a long way from the thick weeds of my early books on French philosophy. I got here thanks to the prompting of two liturgical theologians I count as my teachers. Robert Webber's work had a significant impact on me at a crucial phase of my life, and in many ways I'm simply writing in his wake. This little book is a dinghy bobbing along behind the ship of Webber's "ancient-future" corpus. If I can help a few people board the mother ship, my work here is done.

Closer to home, my colleague and friend John Witvliet is someone who takes joy in fostering the work of others, serving as a catalyst for them to realize a few of the six million ideas John has every day before breakfast (only a few of them being impossible). My thinking on these matters was launched by a mix of questions and challenges from John, who also gave me a bunch of the answers. I dedicate this book to the two of them as a small attempt to repay my debts.

Over the past five years I have enjoyed the hospitality of an incredible array of schools, colleges, universities, churches, and other organizations who have invited me to speak on these themes. This book has bubbled up from those conversations. I'm grateful for the opportunity to think out loud with friends and can recall a hundred scenes with fondness. I had always guessed that books garnered readers; I never realized they would also generate friendships.

Some of those friends very kindly agreed to give up time from their own busy schedules to read a draft of this book. I'm grateful for their charity and honesty, their encouragement and pushback. Thanks go to Matthew Beimers, Darryl De Boer, Mike Cosper, and Rev. Chris Schutte for walking alongside this project. It felt like I had friends with me during the final revisions.

Much of this was written and revised down the street from my house at the Wealthy Street Bakery. Thanks to them for letting me camp out for long afternoons for just the price of a cappuccino (and, every once in a while, a scone—but don't tell Deanna). The soundtrack of the book was channeled through my earbuds on those afternoons: a mix of Jason Isbell's *Southeastern*; the Avett Brothers; the National; and, in the late stages, the brilliant sadness of Sufjan Stevens's *Carrie and Lowell*.

If this book gives you a peek into my life, you'll see that it is a life indelibly shaped by a community of friends and family who have taught me how to love. Mark and Dawn Mulder have been one of the steadiest presences in our life for fifteen years now— friends who are more like family. We're grateful, too, for Gwen and Ryan Genzink, who have walked alongside us and who share our love of good cocktails.

You'll see our children make some appearances in these pages, but you still won't grasp the extent to which they have blessed me. I count it sheer grace that they love me in spite of my foibles and failures.

Above all, looming over and behind and under all of this is Deanna. She has made our home and life an incubator of love. I'm often reminded of something I realized when I visited L'Abri in Switzerland. While it was the philosophical work of Francis Schaeffer that drew me there, anyone who makes the pilgrimage to L'Abri realizes that the ethos out of which his work emerged was nourished by his wife, Edith. She, with her gifts of hospitality, didn't just "support" Francis: she made what he did possible. She cultivated the space of imagination that birthed the vision and ideas (well captured in Edith Schaeffer's history of L'Abri, but also articulated in *The Hidden Art of Homemaking*). So, too, this book emerges from a household that makes it possible: the ideas grew in the soil of Deanna's gardens, have been nourished by her incredible passion for good food, percolated amidst the beauty she has cultivated in our home, and blossomed thanks to her gift of hospitality (code for "wine and cheese!"). The singular grace in my life is being her beloved.

NOTES

Chapter 1 You Are What You Love

1. See Charles Duhigg, *The Power of Habit: Why We Do What We Do in Life and Business* (New York: Random House, 2014).

2. A theme powerfully explored in David Foster Wallace's novel, *Infinite Jest* (Boston: Little, Brown, 1996).

3. Augustine, *Confessions*, trans. Henry Chadwick (Oxford: Oxford University Press, 1992), 1.1.1.

4. Cf. J. I. Packer and Thomas Howard, *Christianity: The True Humanism* (Waco: Word, 1985).

5. Irenaeus, *Against Heresies* 4.20.7.

6. One could say this is mistaking *eros* with *porneia*.

7. Blaise Pascal, *Pensées and Other Writings*, trans. Honor Levi (Oxford: Oxford University Press, 2008), 154.

8. Antoine de Saint-Exupéry, *The Wisdom of the Sands* (New York: Harcourt Brace, 1950).

9. Augustine, *Confessions* 13.9.10.

10. Ibid. Augustine's original references were to the Vulgate: Pss. 83:6; 119:1; and 121:6, respectively. In some ways Eddie Vedder's song "Rise" (on the *Into the Wild* soundtrack, but also very familiar to fans of *Deadliest Catch*) combines both of these metaphors: "Gonna rise up / Find my direction magnetically." (Thanks to Mark Mulder for the reminder.)

11. Aquinas, *Summa Theologica* I–II, 92.1.

12. These same principles hold for acquiring *bad* moral habits as well—namely, vices. So I also learn vice by imitation and by practice. Consider, then, 3 John 11: "Dear friend, do not imitate what is evil but what is good."

13. So too to the Thessalonians: "You became imitators of us and of the Lord, for you welcomed the message in the midst of severe suffering with the joy given by the Holy Spirit" (1 Thess. 1:6; cf. 2 Thess. 3:7, 9).

14. "Monroe Steered by Faulty Compass," *New York Times*, February 12, 1914.

15. Martin Luther, *Luther's Large Catechism*, trans. John Nicholas Lenker (Minneapolis: Luther, 1908), 44.

16. John Calvin, *Institutes* 1.11.8.

17. David Foster Wallace, "Plain Old Untrendy Troubles and Emotions," *The Guardian*, September 20, 2008, 2. A version of this has since been published as *This Is Water: Some Thoughts, Delivered on a Significant Occasion, about Living a Compassionate Life* (New York: Little, Brown, 2009).

Chapter 2 You Might Not Love What You Think

1. In Tarkovsky's Russian Orthodox tradition, Lent is described as a season of "bright sadness."

2. Geoff Dyer, *Zona* (New York: Vintage, 2012), 161.

3. Ibid., 170.

4. Ibid., 165.

5. Ibid., 179, emphasis added.

6. Ibid., 171.

7. Penitential Order I.

8. Donald Justice, "Men at Forty": "Something is filling them, something / That is like the twilight sound / Of the crickets, immense, / Filling the woods at the foot of the slope / Behind their mortgaged houses" (in *Fathers: A Collection of Poems*, ed. David Ray and Judy Ray [New York: St. Martin's Press, 1997], 110).

9. This question was posed to Lester earlier in the film. Lester has been notified that he's being let go from his advertising job of fifteen years. Newly emboldened by his encounter with Ricky Fitts, Lester hints at some private knowledge in his possession that might make the company CEO rather uncomfortable. Brad, the smarmy consultant tasked with firing Lester, understands blackmail when he hears it and simply asks, "What do you want?"

10. See also Daniel Kahneman, *Thinking: Fast and Slow* (New York: Farrar, Straus & Giroux, 2011), and John A. Bargh and Tanya L. Chartrand, "The Unbearable Automaticity of Being," *American Psychologist* 54 (1999): 462–79. For a helpful journalistic overview of this research and its implications, see David Brooks, *The Social Animal: The Hidden Sources of Love, Character, and Achievement* (New York: Random House, 2011).

11. Timothy Wilson, *Strangers to Ourselves: Discovering the Adaptive Unconscious* (Cambridge, MA: Harvard University Press, 2002), 6–7.

12. Brooks, *Social Animal*, 127.

13. Bargh and Chartrand, "Unbearable Automaticity of Being," 468.

14. For a trenchant analysis of stereotypes as a kind of "implicit understanding," see Alexis Shotwell, *Knowing Otherwise: Race, Gender, and Implicit Understanding* (University Park: Penn State University Press, 2011).

15. David Foster Wallace, "Plain Old Untrendy Troubles and Emotions," *The Guardian*, September 20, 2008, 2.

16. The following section appeared in a slightly different form in James K. A. Smith, *Desiring the Kingdom: Worship, Worldview, and Cultural Formation*, Cultural Liturgies 1 (Grand Rapids: Baker Academic, 2009), 20–22.

17. This, it turns out, is not an accident. See Ira Zepp, *The New Religious Image of Urban America: The Shopping Mall as Ceremonial Center* (Boulder: University Press of Colorado, 1997).

18. For a haunting exploration of mannequins as "secular saints," see the short documentary *34x25x36*, in which mannequin creators explicitly invoke worship as the goal of their work. "Barney's is the church of today," they suggest. The film can be viewed at https://www.youtube.com/watch?v=uM-0n Uy7Ye0. My thanks to Bryan Kibbe for pointing me to this a few years back.

19. The Canadian philosopher Charles Taylor talks about "social imaginaries" rather than "worldviews" in order to honor the fact that this way of approaching the world is more on the order of the imagination than the intellect. A social imaginary, he says, is "much broader and deeper than the intellectual schemes people may entertain when they *think* about social reality in a disengaged mode" (Taylor, *Modern Social Imaginaries* [Durham, NC: Duke University Press, 2004], 23, emphasis added). The social imaginary is "the way ordinary people 'imagine' their social surroundings," he points out. This is "not expressed in theoretical terms, but is carried in images, stories, and legends" (ibid.).

20. For a literary skewering of this, see Tom Wolfe's novel *I Am Charlotte Simmons* (New York: Farrar, Straus & Giroux, 2004).

21. For a succinct encapsulation of this biblical vision of *shalom*, see Nicholas Wolterstorff, *Until Justice and Peace Embrace* (Grand Rapids: Eerdmans, 1983), 69–72.

22. Jean Kilbourne's *Killing Us Softly* documentaries argue that advertising particularly heightens competition between women, and not only for the attention of men. A caricature of this intragender competition might be found in the 2004 film *Mean Girls*.

23. Granted, I think many renditions of Christian worship—reflecting what we might call "refueling" models—are subject to the same disappointments and frustrations.

24. Roddy Scheer and Doug Moss, "Use It and Lose It: The Outsize Effect of U.S. Consumption on the Environment," *Scientific American*, September 14, 2012, http://www.scientificamerican.com/article/american-consumption-habits.

25. For a lucid introduction to Christian formation through this lens, see Rebecca Konyndyk DeYoung, *The Glittering Vices: A New Look at the Seven Deadly Sins and Their Remedies* (Grand Rapids: Brazos, 2009).

26. For a helpful introduction to this spiritual discipline, see http://www
.ignatianspirituality.com/ignatian-prayer/the-examen/.

Chapter 3 The Spirit Meets You Where You Are

1. See Brian Wansink, *Mindless Eating: Why We Eat More Than We Think*
(New York: Bantam, 2007), and Michael Pollan, *The Omnivore's Dilemma*
(New York: Penguin, 2007).

2. The following section appeared in a slightly different form in James
K. A. Smith, *Imagining the Kingdom: How Worship Works*, Cultural Liturgies 2 (Grand Rapids: Baker Academic, 2013), 8–10.

3. In some ways, this much conscious intentionality is required only because I had built up a lifetime of bad habits that needed to be undone;
someone *raised* in such healthy rhythms would, in fact, acquire good tastes
and hungers without much consciousness at all.

4. Matthew Myers Boulton, *Life in God: John Calvin, Practical Formation, and the Future of Protestant Theology* (Grand Rapids: Eerdmans,
2011), 229–30.

5. For a wise articulation of this point, see Michael Horton, *Ordinary:
Sustainable Faith in a Radical, Restless World* (Grand Rapids: Zondervan,
2014).

6. Dallas Willard, *The Spirit of the Disciplines* (San Francisco: Harper-
One, 1999).

7. Craig Dykstra, *Growing in the Life of Faith*, 2nd ed. (Louisville: Westminster John Knox, 2005), 67, 63.

8. Marva Dawn, *Reaching Out without Dumbing Down* (Grand Rapids:
Eerdmans, 1995), 79.

9. Nicholas Wolterstorff, "The Reformed Liturgy," in *Major Themes in
the Reformed Tradition*, ed. Donald McKim (Grand Rapids: Eerdmans,
1992), 287, 288. He calls this "a sacramentalism of God's static presence"
rather than one "of God's active doing."

10. Ibid., 290–91, emphasis original.

11. Calvin, Commentary on Galatians 5:3, quoted in John Witvliet, *Worship Seeking Understanding: Windows into Christian Practice* (Grand Rapids:
Baker Academic, 2003), 145. Witvliet notes "an exact correlation" of Calvin's
"notion of divine agency in worship . . . with Calvin's soteriological structure. . . . Part of the enduring appeal of Calvin's theology of liturgy is that
his position was carefully worked out in conversation with and in terms of
an entire theological system" (in *Worship Seeking Understanding*, 147n74).

12. Hughes Oliphant Old, "John Calvin and the Prophetic Criticism of
Worship," in *John Calvin and the Church: A Prism of Reform*, ed. Timothy
George (Louisville: Westminster John Knox, 1990), 234.

13. Nicholas Wolterstorff, "Reflections on Kuyper's *Our Worship*," an
appendix to Abraham Kuyper, *Our Worship*, ed. Harry Boonstra (Grand

Rapids: Eerdmans, 2009), 358, emphasis original to Kuyper; quotes within this quote are from *Our Worship*, 171 and 283, respectively. At the conclusion of this piece, Wolterstorff remarks, "I had not read Kuyper's *Our Worship* until I did so for these reflections. There are some things in Kuyper's discussion that I would want to dissociate myself from. But as to the central idea and its implications, I now feel that almost everything I have written about liturgy in the past amounts to reinventing the wheel" (ibid., 360).

14. Philip Butin, *Revelation, Redemption, Response: Calvin's Trinitarian Understanding of the Divine-Human Relationship* (New York: Oxford University Press, 1995), 102, quoted in Witvliet, *Worship Seeking Understanding*, 146.

15. Jeremy Begbie is one of our wisest guides in this territory. See Jeremy Begbie, *Resounding Truth: Christian Wisdom in the World of Music* (Grand Rapids: Baker Academic, 2007), and Jeremy S. Begbie and Steven R. Guthrie, eds., *Resonant Witness: Conversations between Music and Theology* (Grand Rapids: Eerdmans, 2011).

16. Oscar Wilde, "The Critic as Artist," in *The Portable Oscar Wilde*, ed. Stanley Weintraub (Hammondsworth, UK: Penguin, 1981), 76.

Chapter 4 What Story Are You In?

1. In the sense that Chip Heath and Dan Heath mean in *Made to Stick: Why Some Ideas Survive and Others Die* (New York: Random House, 2007).

2. In other words, Cranmer's convictions were both evangelical *and* "catholic": "[C. S.] Lewis notes that Cranmer and the other makers of the prayer book 'wished their book to be praised not for original genius but for catholicity and antiquity'" (Alan Jacobs, *The Book of Common Prayer: A Biography* [Princeton: Princeton University Press, 2013], 66).

3. Eamon Duffy, *The Stripping of the Altars: Traditional Religion in England, 1400–1580*, 2nd ed. (New Haven: Yale University Press, 2005), 593, quoted in Jacobs, *Book of Common Prayer*, 59.

4. Jacobs provides a marvelous literary analysis of just *how* the Book of Common Prayer's language works "aesthetically," one might say, pointing to the effect of allusion, alliteration, and "the additive power of parataxis" in Cranmer's strings of conjunctions that roll off the tongue so willingly (*Book of Common Prayer*, 62). He also notes that Cranmer was particularly attuned to how language works communally and audibly: "For it was surely congregational worship that Cranmer had primarily in mind when shaping the words of this book: his English is meant to find its fullest life when said aloud, in unison, the *vox populi* made the organ on which this verbal music shall be played" (ibid., 63–64).

5. See Henri de Lubac, *The Mystery of the Supernatural*, trans. Rosemary Sheed (New York: Crossroad, 1998), 130–37.

6. N. T. Wright, *After You Believe: Why Christian Character Matters* (San Francisco: HarperOne, 2012), 25.

7. Ibid., 26.

8. Alasdair MacIntyre, *After Virtue: A Study in Moral Theory*, 2nd ed. (Notre Dame, IN: University of Notre Dame Press, 1984), 216.

9. James Wood, *How Fiction Works* (New York: Farrar, Straus & Giroux, 2008), 237–38, citing Brigid Lowe, *Victorian Fiction and the Insights of Sympathy* (London: Anthem, 2007), 82–83.

10. Michael W. Goheen and Craig Bartholomew, *The True Story of the Whole World: Finding Your Place in the Biblical Drama* (Grand Rapids: Faith Alive, 2009). Their title riffs on N. T. Wright's claim in *The New Testament and the People of God* (Minneapolis: Fortress, 2009), 41–42: "The whole point of Christianity is that it offers a story which is the story of the whole world. It is public truth."

11. C. S. Lewis, "They Asked for a Paper," in *Is Theology Poetry?* (London: Geoffrey Bless, 1962), 164–65.

12. What follows doesn't even pretend to be a comprehensive theology of worship but is rather an invitation to see historic worship in a new way. For more fulsome introductions to intentional, historic worship, see, for example, Robert Webber, *Ancient-Future Worship: Proclaiming and Enacting God's Narrative* (Grand Rapids: Baker Books, 2008); Bryan Chapell, *Christ-Centered Worship: Letting the Gospel Shape Our Practice* (Grand Rapids: Baker Academic, 2009); Mike Cosper, *Rhythms of Grace: How the Church's Worship Tells the Story of the Gospel* (Wheaton: Crossway, 2013); Michael Horton, *A Better Way: Rediscovering the Drama of God-Centered Worship* (Grand Rapids: Baker Books, 2003). For a lucid introduction and resources to put all of this into practice, see *The Worship Sourcebook: A Classic Resource for Today's Church*, 2nd ed. (Grand Rapids: Faith Alive / Baker Books, 2013).

13. In *Imagining the Kingdom: How Worship Works*, Cultural Liturgies 2 (Grand Rapids: Baker Academic, 2013), 170–71, I reproduce a table from Frank Senn's monumental work *Christian Liturgy: Catholic and Evangelical* (Minneapolis: Fortress, 1997) that shows the narrative continuity of historic, "catholic" worship across a range of Christian traditions (Roman Catholic, Lutheran, Anglican, Methodist, and Presbyterian/Reformed).

14. This is the pattern of my Reformed tradition. In those Christian traditions that celebrate the Lord's Supper weekly, confession is incorporated into the Eucharistic liturgy.

15. Stanley Hauerwas, *With the Grain of the Universe* (Grand Rapids: Brazos, 2001), drawing on a metaphor suggested by John Howard Yoder.

16. Charles Taylor, *A Secular Age* (Cambridge, MA: Belknap Press of Harvard University Press, 2007), 279–88. For further discussion, see James K. A. Smith, *How (Not) to Be Secular: Reading Charles Taylor* (Grand Rapids: Eerdmans, 2014), 57–59.

17. See Martin Tel and John Witvliet, eds., *Psalms for All Seasons: A Complete Psalter for Worship* (Grand Rapids: Brazos, 2012).

18. David Foster Wallace, "Federer Both Flesh and Not," in *Both Flesh and Not: Essays* (New York: Little, Brown, 2012), 23–24.

19. See Peter Jonker's new book on preaching from a "controlling image," *Preaching in Pictures: Using Images for Sermons That Connect* (Nashville: Abingdon, 2015).

Chapter 5 Guard Your Heart

1. Hans Urs von Balthasar, *Love Alone Is Credible*, trans. D. C. Schindler (San Francisco: Ignatius, 2004), 76. My thanks to Mark Bowald for this book, which has been an ongoing gift.

2. Ibid.

3. Isaiah also suggests the image of God as a nursing mother: "Can a mother forget the baby at her breast and have no compassion on the child she has borne? Though she may forget, I will not forget you!" (Isa. 49:15).

4. James Olthuis, *The Beautiful Risk: A New Psychology of Loving and Being Loved* (Grand Rapids: Zondervan, 2001).

5. For reasons that I hope will become clear below, I try to use the word "household" and not just "home" because I don't want to fall into a narrow picture that assumes we are all parents. God calls some of us to singleness (1 Cor. 7:8), and not all of us live in parent-child homes. There can be all sorts of different "households" that are faithful sites of Christian formation. Indeed, I think it is crucial that those of us who inhabit families make room for sisters and brothers who are single, recognizing that there are many ways to be a household.

6. David Matzko McCarthy, *Sex and Love in the Home*, new ed. (London: SCM, 2004), 93–97.

7. I won't argue for paedobaptism here (a mode of baptism shared across a number of traditions). My analysis assumes it but is also relevant to believers' baptism in many ways. For a conversation that looks for overlapping consensus, see John H. Armstrong, ed., *Understanding Four Views on Baptism* (Grand Rapids: Zondervan, 2007).

8. Peter Leithart, *The Priesthood of the Plebs: A Theology of Baptism* (Eugene, OR: Wipf and Stock, 2003), 210.

9. Christian Reformed Church Service for Baptism (1981) in the *Psalter Hymnal*, 955.

10. I've always thought this is an important reason *not* to have grandpa or grandma, who might be a pastor elsewhere, "parachute in" to baptize a grandchild. It signals *in practice* that the bloodlines of kin have some significance in the body of Christ. This is not to erode the "natural" family, of course, just to relativize it—and baptism is one of the prime rites that does so.

11. Alexander Schmemann, *For the Life of the World: Sacraments and Orthodoxy* (Crestwood, NY: St. Vladimir's Seminary Press, 1973), 90.

12. David Matzko McCarthy, *The Good Life: Genuine Christianity for the Middle Class* (Grand Rapids: Brazos, 2004), 52.

13. Schmemann, *For the Life of the World*, 90.

14. See the astute analysis of McCarthy in *Sex and Love in the Home*, 93–97.

15. Ibid., 111.

16. McCarthy, *Good Life*, 52.

17. Ibid.

18. On disruptive friendships, see ibid., 35–37.

19. *Divorce Corp*, http://www.divorcecorp.com.

20. See, for example, "The Sacrament of Holy Matrimony," http://www.antiochian.org/midwest/holy-matrimony.

21. Schmemann, *For the Life of the World*, 88.

22. Ibid., 89.

23. Ibid.

24. Ibid., 89–90.

25. This is a reason to value multigenerational worship, where families worship together as a whole rather than sequestering children in an expressivist experience somewhere else in the church.

26. On this score, there is a lot of wisdom to be gained by returning to the Westminster Divines' "Directory for Family Worship," a supplement to their "Directory for the Publick Worship of God."

27. Michael Horton, *A Better Way: Rediscovering the Drama of God-Centered Worship* (Grand Rapids: Baker Books, 2003).

28. You might also consider making the family calendar on the side of the fridge a liturgical calendar like the *Salt of the Earth* calendar produced by the University Hill United Church in Vancouver, British Columbia (see www.thechristiancalendar.com) or the *St. James Calendar of the Christian Year* produced by the Fellowship of St. James (see www.fsj.org).

29. Etienne Wenger, *Communities of Practice: Learning, Meaning, and Identity* (New York: Cambridge University Press, 1998), 176.

30. Norman Wirzba helpfully points out that "Sabbath" is not synonymous with "doing nothing." See *Living the Sabbath: Discovering the Rhythms of Rest and Delight* (Grand Rapids: Brazos, 2006).

Chapter 6 Teach Your Children Well

1. Stanley Hauerwas, *State of the University* (Oxford: Wiley, 2007), 46.

2. There has been much hand-wringing of late about the state of youth religion and spirituality today, crystallized in Christian Smith's study *Soul Searching: The Religious and Spiritual Lives of American Teenagers*, with Melinda Lunquist Denton (New York: Oxford University Press, 2005). Smith

laments the sad state of catechesis in Christian communities where young people adhere to what he calls "moralistic therapeutic deism" rather than orthodox Christian confession. There are legitimate concerns here, but I would note that many of Smith's measures are decidedly "intellectualist." Cf. Kenda Creasy Dean, *Almost Christian: What the Faith of Our Teenagers Is Telling the American Church* (New York: Oxford University Press, 2010).

3. This brief chapter doesn't pretend to be comprehensive. For more sustained reflection on a liturgical approach to education, see James K. A. Smith, *Desiring the Kingdom: Worship, Worldview, and Cultural Formation*, Cultural Liturgies 1 (Grand Rapids: Baker Academic, 2009), and David I. Smith and James K. A. Smith, eds., *Teaching and Christian Practices: Reshaping Faith and Learning* (Grand Rapids: Eerdmans, 2011).

4. For more information, see Sofia Cavalletti, *The Religious Potential of the Child* (Chicago: Liturgy Training Publications, 1992), and Sofia Cavalletti, Patricia Coulter, Gianna Gobbi, and Silvana Q. Montanaro, *The Good Shepherd and the Child: A Joyful Journey* (Chicago: Liturgy Training Publications, 2007). Also visit http://www.cgsusa.org/about/.

5. See Kevin Adams, *150: Finding Your Story in the Psalms* (Grand Rapids: Faith Alive, 2011), which well articulates why the Psalms are an ancient gift for the contemporary church.

6. Phyllis Tickle, *The Divine Hours*, is helpfully available in a pocket edition (New York: Oxford University Press, 2007).

7. And obviously, as with adults, liturgical catechesis (understanding why we do what we do when we worship) is crucial to young people's growing understanding of the faith.

8. Craig Dykstra, *Growing in the Life of Faith*, 2nd ed. (Louisville: Westminster John Knox, 2005). See also Dallas Willard, *The Spirit of the Disciplines* (San Francisco: HarperOne, 1999).

9. Dorothy Bass and Don Richter, *Way to Live: Christian Practices for Teens* (Nashville: Upper Room Books, 2002). See also Andrew Root, *Bonhoeffer as Youth Worker: A Theological Vision for Discipleship and Life Together* (Grand Rapids: Baker Academic, 2014).

10. There are a host of ways this can go wrong—for example, when suburban "service" is framed as "inner city" ministry (= white kids' *noblesse oblige* for "urban" [i.e., African American] neighborhoods) or when service is turned into "short-term mission trips" that are just opportunities for privileged youth to spend spring break in the Caribbean, etc. For wisdom on these matters, consult Robert J. Priest, ed., *Effective Engagement in Short-Term Missions: Doing It Right!* (Pasadena, CA: William Carey Library, 2012).

11. For an argument along these lines, with case studies of pedagogical experiments drawing on historic Christian practices, see Smith and Smith, *Teaching and Christian Practices*.

12. My thanks to Darryl De Boer for sharing this vision in detail. My sketch here depends on his own summary.

13. James Davison Hunter, *The Death of Character: Moral Education in an Age without Good or Evil* (New York: Basic Books, 2000), 215.

14. Steven R. Guthrie, "The Wisdom of Song," in *Resonant Witness: Conversations between Music and Theology*, ed. Jeremy S. Begbie and Steven R. Guthrie (Grand Rapids: Eerdmans, 2011), 400.

15. For discussion of the practices of Christian hospitality, see Ana María Pineda, "Hospitality," in *Practicing Our Faith: A Way of Life for a Searching People*, ed. Dorothy C. Bass, 2nd ed. (San Francisco: Jossey-Bass, 2010), 29–42; Christine D. Pohl, *Making Room: Recovering Hospitality as a Christian Tradition* (Grand Rapids: Eerdmans, 1999); and David Smith and Barbara Carvill, *The Gift of the Stranger: Faith, Hospitality, and Foreign Language Learning* (Grand Rapids: Eerdmans, 2000).

16. See Smith and Smith, *Teaching and Christian Practices*.

17. Published in the Raccolta #764, Pius XI Studiorum Ducem, 1923.

Chapter 7 You Make What You Want

1. For a helpful elucidation of this point, see Norman Wirzba, *From Nature to Creation: A Christian Vision for Understanding the World*, The Church and Postmodern Culture (Grand Rapids: Baker Academic, 2015).

2. For a lucid discussion of this narrative continuity from Genesis 1 to Revelation 22, see J. Richard Middleton, *A New Heaven and a New Earth: Reclaiming Biblical Eschatology* (Grand Rapids: Baker Academic, 2014).

3. J. Richard Middleton, *The Liberating Image: The Imago Dei in Genesis 1* (Grand Rapids: Brazos, 2005), 60.

4. J. R. R. Tolkien, *Tree and Leaf* (San Francisco: HarperCollins, 2001), 37.

5. James Davison Hunter, *To Change the World: The Irony, Tragedy, and Possibility of Christianity in the Late Modern World* (New York: Oxford University Press, 2010).

6. He sometimes claimed that he had sketched the whole narrative out in a "Journal of the Whills," but Chris Taylor's research points out this too is a fiction.

7. Cass R. Sunstein, "How Star Wars Illuminates Constitutional Law (and Authorship)," review of *How Star Wars Conquered the Universe: The Past, Present, and Future of a Multibillion Dollar Franchise*, by Chris Taylor, *The New Rambler Review*, http://newramblerreview.com/book-reviews/fiction-literature/how-star-wars-illuminates-constitutional-law-and-authorship. Quotes throughout this section are from this review.

8. One could point to influential articulations of this, such as Charles Colson and Nancy Pearcey, *How Now Shall We Live?* (Carol Stream, IL: Tyndale, 1999), and Andy Crouch, *Culture Making: Recovering Our Creative Calling* (Downers Grove, IL: InterVarsity, 2008).

9. Gabe Lyons, *The Next Christians: Seven Ways You Can Live the Gospel and Restore the World* (Colorado Springs: Multnomah, 2012).

10. Herbert A. Simon, "The Science of Design: Creating the Artificial," *Design Issues* 4, no. 1/2 (1988), quoted in Robert Grudin, *Design and Truth* (New Haven: Yale University Press, 2010), 3.

11. Grudin, *Design and Truth*, 4.

12. Ibid., 8.

13. Ibid., 7.

14. Martin Filler, "Victory!," *New York Review of Books* 59 (July 12, 2012): 14–18. Subsequent quotes throughout this section are from this article.

15. Alvin Plantinga, "Advice to Christian Philosophers," *Faith and Philosophy* 1, no. 3 (1984): 253–71.

Benediction

1. Alexander Schmemann, *For the Life of the World: Sacraments and Orthodoxy* (Crestwood, NY: St. Vladimir's Seminary Press, 1973), 29.

INDEX